SECULARISM, COMMUNALISM AND THE INTELLECTU-

Secularism, Communalism and the Intellectuals

Zaheer Baber

Three Essays
COLLECTIVE

Second Edition January 2026

ISBN 978-81-88789-47-4

Three Essays
COLLECTIVE

B-957 Palam Vihar, GURGAON 122 017 India
Phone: 0 9868126587, 0 98683 44843
info@threeessays.com Website: www.threeessays.com
Printed at Replika Press Pvt. Ltd., India

For Anissa

CONTENTS

PREFACE

The demolition of the mosque in Ayodhya and the carnage that enveloped the country in its aftermath generated enough frenzied bigotry to propel the ideology of *Hindutva* to the centre-stage of politics and the public sphere in India. Just a few years prior to this watershed event, the idea that the BJP would ever be in power at the centre was unthinkable. However, the incendiary communal can of worms opened by the court decision on Ayodhya and exploited to the hilt by the Congress government under Rajiv Gandhi paved the way for the mainstreaming of communal politics. Up until that point, the various iterations of Hindutva doctrines connected to a wide range of political organizations and personalities had at best a very tenuous purchase on the political landscape and discourse. Although majoritarian communalist views within the Congress were always present, they were of limited consequence, hedged in as they were by the dominant ethos of secularism. A significant opening up of the communalist space occurred during the period of the Emergency. Under the autocratic rule initiated by Mrs. Gandhi, prisons emerged as the premier sites for an extremely ideological diverse coalition of bedfellows. The coming to power of the Janata Party, although short-lived, provided the first opportunity for hard-core communalists to be in positions of institutional state power. The demise of the monopoly the Congress had on state power at the Centre contributed to the emergence of new national and regional political parties and the rejuvenation and renaming of existing ones. The resultant jockeying for power at the Centre effected through the organized orchestration and exploitation of serial bouts of communal and chauvinistic-nationalistic frenzies around events connected with Kashmir, Punjab, Nellie, Meerut, Ayodhya, Shah Bano, Mandal and more recently Gujarat, contributed to the mainstreaming of previously stigmatized communal ideologies. The struggles over the ballot box were frequently expressed via bullets and a wide variety of indigenous blood-letting devices.

The causes and consequences of these depressing events need not detain us here. They have been admirably documented and analyzed by many scholars just as they have been creatively distorted by communalists with tragically violent results. Although some tentative explanations are offered in the narrative that follows, the main focus of this monograph is an attempt to come to grips with the inadvertent but very real role of some very prominent intellectuals in contributing to the creation of conditions and space for the mainstreaming of communalism in India over the past two decades or so. The transformation of communalism from a defensive mode to an unapologetic, assertive one has of course been helped along by a number of structural and ideological transformations. Only somebody saturated with unadulterated intellectual hubris can dream of claiming all the credit for the communalization of Indian society. However at particular structural and political conjunctures, the purchase of ideas produced by professional intellectuals goes beyond the usual careerist promotion and tenure decisions. This has been especially true in the case of India where the intellectual discussions and debates in the dailies have been of a very high calibre. The vilification of prominent historians such as Romila Thapar, and the selective, politicized editing of textbooks to create mythographies indicate that ideas have real and sometime tragically depressing consequences. And while there is no doubt that the intellectuals whose ideas are discussed in the first chapter have been unambiguously non-communal in their views, their fashionable and smug critiques and outright dismissals of modernity, rationality and secularism have dovetailed rather dramatically and tragically with the ascendancy of the BJP to power at the Centre.

The shock defeat of the NDA that was the fig-leaf for the BJP and the entire Sangh Parivar provides some space for cautious optimism. However, this optimism ought not to be blown out of proportion. In the past, the Congress and the BJP have successfully adopted each other's strategy during their battles for the ballot. Both parties, driven by the exigencies of political calculations switched between communal and economic issues as their election platforms. Immersed in the game of political strategizing, the BJP and the Congress have frequently taken turns to act as each other's alter egos. The popularity of a party like the BJP is partly attributable to the willingness of the Congress to effectively flirt with communal issues at particular political conjunctures. However, although the Congress has sometimes sought alliances with communal parties such as the Indian Union Muslim League in Kerala, it is not organically linked to unambiguously communal organizations analogous to the Sangh Parivar. The first response of the VHP and RSS to the shock defeat of the BJP and its NDA coalition was to lay the blame on what was termed as the "abandonment of the *Hindutva* agenda". However anyone who has followed the determined re-writing of history text-books, the introduction of Vedic science and mathematics in the curriculum, the concerted attacks on eminent historians and the nuclear detonations within weeks of assuming the helm of a shaky coalition will fail to notice any abandonment of *Hindutva* as a long-term goal (Nanda, 2002; 2003). What the BJP did realize of course was that communal frenzies cannot be sustained for extended periods of time. Massacres and demolition of mosques may deliver the required votes and contribute to the main-streaming of communal prejudice, but they cannot ever become full-time occupations. Despite the shock defeat of the BJP at the Centre, the electoral gain cynically extracted from the genocide in Gujarat was widely held up as a model that could be, under the right conditions, emulated elsewhere. Atal Bihari Vajpayee, consistently anointed by the media as the "moderate", "humane", almost the non-communal face of the BJP had this to say about the lessons of Gujarat at the party congress in 2002:

> What happened in Gujarat? If a conspiracy had not been hatched to burn alive the innocent passengers of the Sabarmati Express, then the subsequent tragedy in Gujarat could have been averted. But this did not happen. People were torched alive. Who were those culprits? The government is investigating into this. Intelligence agencies are collecting all the information. But we should not forget how the tragedy of Gujarat started. The subsequent developments were no doubt condemnable, but who lit the fire? How did the fire spread? . . . . Wherever Muslims live, they don't like to live in co-existence with others, they don't like to mingle with others; and instead of propagating their ideas in a peaceful manner, they want to spread their faith by resorting to terror and threats. The world has become alert to this danger (cited in

Nussbaum 2003).

In the aftermath of the decisive defeat of the BJP led NDA coalition, it is quite likely that the so-called moderate faction of the BJP will be subdued and even pushed aside. The possibility of more communal conflicts designed to reassert the *Hindutva* agenda is all too real. One of the most dramatic social consequences of the ascendancy of the BJP was the mainstreaming of communal prejudice. Before the electoral victories of the BJP, many individuals were quite embarrassed and defensive about their communal proclivities. Some would claim that they were voting for the party, simply because it represented an alternative to the Congress. With the consolidation of the BJP's power at the centre, this critical mass of individuals had become comfortable with their communal prejudices. It is unlikely that the Sangh Parivar strategists will simply sit back and let these born again overt communalists melt back into their latent communal selves. If the current Congress led coalition begins to falter, larger numbers of latent communalists will once again become the targets of both BJP and the Congress for their respective sectarian, destructive projects for the nation.

Various versions of the chapters that follow were earlier presented as papers at a number of conferences. These include, the ASEAN Inter-University Conference, Cebu City (1995); the *International Sociological Association's* World Congress of Sociology in Montreal (1998); the annual meetings of the *American Sociological Association* in Chicago (1999) and the *International Sociological Association's* conference at Hitotsubashi University in Tokyo (2003). I am grateful to the participants at these conferences who provided feedback, encouragement and sometimes discouraging critiques. Different versions and sections of the material included here have also appeared in the following journals: *Sociology: Journal of the British Sociological Association*; *Dialectical An-*

thropology, and *Journal of Contemporary Asia.* Many individuals directly commented and engaged with the issues raised here. They include: Michal Bodemann, Chris Bonastia, Craig Calhoun, Frances Hasso, James Jasper, Rajive McMullen, Sourayan Mookerjee, Ali Javed, Maritsa Poros, Howard Winant, Gregory Clancey, Mukul Ranjan, John Whalen-Bridge, Ravi Vaitheespara, Abdul Jamil Urfi, Isaka Riho and Yoshiko Ashiwa. Given the nature and tone of this book, it is important to emphasize the fact that none of them necessarily agrees with any of the contentious ideas presented here.

Zaheer Baber

SECULARISM, ANTI-SECULARISM AND "THEORETICAL BUBBLE-BLOWING"

> *[Secularism is an] alien cultural ideology...a gift of Chris-tianity...an impossible credo of life [it is] impractical as a basis for state action...impotent as a blueprint for the future.* T.N. Madan (1987:748-49)

> *To accept the ideology of secularism is to accept the ideologies of progress and modernity as the new justification of domination, and the use of violence to achieve and sustain ideologies as the new opiates of the masses.* Ashis Nandy (1988:192)

> *The principle of secularism basically demands symmetric treatment of different religious communities in politics and in the affairs of the state. It is not obvious why such symmetric treatment must somehow involve "the use of violence to achieve and sustain ideologies as the new opiates of the masses"....There are good reasons to resist the contrary enticements that have been so plentifully offered recently. The winter of our discontent might not be giving away, right now, to a glorious summer, but the abandonment of secularism would make things far more wintry than they currently are.* Amartya Sen (1996:37-43)

Marx may or may not have been justified in describing religion as the "opium of the masses", but anti-secularism has emerged as the new opium of some elite intellectuals writing on India. In this chapter, the role of these intellectuals in producing the theoretical space for the subsequent ascendancy of the political forces associated with the Sangh Parivar is mapped out. In the wake of increasing communal strife in India, a new consensus over the status and possible future of secularism has emerged. Since many intellectuals writing about the issue have been fairly candid about their views, there seems to be little risk of oversimplifying or misrepresenting their position. Their arguments can be stated without any fear of ambiguity. In the Indian context, secularism as a policy has failed, will continue to fail, because it represents a "Western" conceptual conceit that cannot be applied to "Eastern" societies. Given the quite different cultural context of its genesis, it was foolhardy of Nehru and other "Westernized" leaders of his generation to foist secularism on an utterly alien social and cultural milieu. Not only are policies based on secularist principles unlikely to work in the Indian context, but attempts to force such alien ideologies on a society that is fundamentally religious in nature has had the pernicious unintended consequence of actually encouraging communal conflicts in contemporary India. The damage inflicted by the adoption of policies emanating from alien contexts can however be contained and even reversed provided it is recognized that "Western" concepts like secularism are counterproductive. Secularism as a policy has had the effect of draining out the last vestiges of religiosity from public life. The only remedy against endemic communal conflict is the injection of heavy doses of religious values into the public sphere. Such a policy is the only hope for restoring the alleged communal tranquillity of pre-colonial Indian society, before secularism and other alien ideas and practices were introduced by the colonial Trojan horse. Curiously enough, although a vast majority of the anti-secularist writers are trained as sociologists or anthropologists, they fail to deploy any sociological insights while examining the Indian situation. Although, predictably enough, they view the communal issue in India through the inevitable and unambiguous "crisis of modernity" lens, they refuse to seriously engage with the work of scholars who have actually offered sociologically grounded accounts of the emergence of secular ideas and institutions. Thus, the numerous writings and reflections of sociologists like Robert Bellah (1970; 1980), Bryan Wilson (1969), Frank Lechner (1991) are not deemed fit for serious engagement, while quasi-philosophical pronouncements and grand, one-dimensional theorizing on a really grand scale about the curse of modernity are mobilized to push for the death of secularism.

At the forefront of scholars who question the adequacy of secularism as a policy and who suggest its abandonment in the light of what they interpret as nothing but failure, is T. N. Madan. In the early nineties Madan (1994: 1095) launched an "acerbic ideological attack on secularism" in an article with the revealing title of *Secularism in its Place* (Madan 1987). In this piece Madan staked the curious claim that secularism was bound to fail in India because it constitutes an "alien cultural ideology", "a gift of Christianity", "an impossible credo of life" that is "impractical as a basis for state action" and "impotent as a blueprint for the future" (Madan 1987:748-49). Secularism is apparently "impotent as a blueprint for the future because, by its very nature, it is incapable of countering religious fundamentalism and fanaticism." It is also "impossible as a credo of life because the great majority of the people of South Asia are in their own eyes active adherents of some religious faith" (Madan 1987:748). As Madan would have us believe, the processes of structural transformation of societies need to be ignored, and secularism should be seen as nothing more than "the dream of a minority which wants to shape the majority in its own image, which wants to impose its will upon history but lacks the power to do so under a democratically organized polity" (Madan 1987:748). Secularism moreover, is simply part and parcel of a larger package, the dreaded phenomenon of "modernity" that, horror of horrors, has sinister designs for the "enlargement of human freedom and the enhancement of the range of choices open to a people in respect to things that matter, including their present and future life-styles" (Madan 1987:748). In a barely concealed burst of nostalgia that obviously colours his evaluation of the past, Madan asserts categorically that "there are no fundamentalists or revivalists in traditional society" and devotes the rest of his article to a critique of the "modernist minority in India" that exhibits "moral arrogance" in trying to "stigmatize the majority as primordially oriented and to preach secularism to the latter as the law of human existence" (Madan 1987: 749). Communal violence, as Madan would have us believe, is a direct consequence of the actions of this arrogant secularist and modernist, because he happens to know that "in truth it is the marginalization of religious faith, which is what secularization is, that permits the perversion of religion" (Madan 1987:749).

In a more recent contribution, some earlier formulations are retracted but Madan continues to focus on apparent doctrinal differences between Christianity and other religions to contend that the "Hindu tradition does not provide us with a dualistic view of the kind which Christianity does." This is apparently so because the "Christian distinction between the sacred and secular domains (two kingdoms, two cities, two swords etc) is widely held to have contributed to the success of the modern ideology in the West" (Madan 1994: 1906). Ignoring social structures completely, Madan feels that such cultural and theological differences are sufficient enough to explain why "a Hindu or a Sikh, or a Muslim for that matter, would find it more difficult to make sense of the notion of privatisation of religion, than perhaps a Christian does" (Madan 1994:1096). Hence, it is hardly surprising that the ideology of secularism, born apparently in an 'alien" and Western context of Christianity is having a rough time in the dramatically different cultural and religious context of India. Madan is certainly not the only scholar who has attacked secularism, but he has certainly contributed substantially to the bandwagon effect that continues to thrive.

Although the intellectuals' rush for a seat on the anti-secularist bandwagon is a relatively recent development, it threatens to wreck the erstwhile consensus among those who analyze Indian society. For scholars, and there are still a few of them around, who are not yet convinced that the rising fortunes of the BJP family combined with recurring bouts of communal blood-letting conclusively establish the spectacular failure of secularism as an ideal and starting ground for realistic policy-making, the rising tide of anti-secularist views amongst intellectuals represents an alarming trend. In the present context of totalising postmodern orthodoxies, the recent writings of Andre Beteille (1994) and Amartaya Sen (1993; 1995) represent the avante-garde of critical reflection at a number of levels. In addition to holding out against the easy dismissal of every vestige of the much maligned modernity, both valorize lucidity. Those who have followed, and it is no easy task to avoid it, the results of the compulsive imperative for the proliferation of an endless array of neologisms or the invevitable tacking on of the prefix "post" to just about anything, will no doubt welcome the lucidity which is at a premium. For unlike the generalized and seductive trend of "turning to the latest fads, exegesis of the pronunciamentos of the most recently crowned idol, chasing the themes everyone else chases at the moment, only to join another hunt before the former is over, always following the loundest barking hound" (Bauman 1987:4), both Beteille and Sen believe that they have something to add to the conversation on the future of Indian society, and they are unwilling to hide their views behind a facade of the latest buys from the ever expanding academic market for fashionable, perennially on the cutting-edge terminologies and neologisms.

In the prevailing intellectual and political context where "secularist" is readily deployed as a term of abuse and differences in religious doctrines are being held causally responsible for communal conflict in India, Beteille's (1994) genuinely socio-logical discussion of the complexities surrounding the concept and practice of secularism is particularly welcome. His distinction between "secularisation" as a social process and "secularism" as an ideology, and his contention, in the course of a critique of Madan's views, that the former cannot always be attributed to the actions of a "minority of intellectuals determined to impose their will on the unsuspecting masses of people" should hardly elicit objections from any sociologist except those who are committed to an uncompromising culturalism. Making the quite un-fashionable confession that his "own bias, both as an intellectual and as a person, is for secularism", Beteille argues that "consciously-designed ideologies do contribute something to social change, [but] they do not contribute everything", and that "secularisation is not the outcome of that ideology alone, but of a variety of material forces in addition" (1994: 559;561). Although Beteille's observation should constitute a truism for all careful sociologists, it is one that some scholars need to be reminded of, especially in view of the prevailing dogma that endemic communal violence in contemporary India can be attributed primarily, perhaps even solely, to the theory and practice of the "alien" and "western" ideology of secularism.

In response to Beteille's judicious and rather charitable

critique of prevailing dogmas, T. N. Madan (1994) is curiously defensive and claims to have been quoted out of context from his *Secularism in its Place* (1987) article. Beating a hasty retreat, Madan now claims that his article attacking secularism in India was meant to deliver nothing more than a severe jolt to "complacent secularists" who apparently were in a state of collective trance induced by the "mantra [of secularism] given by Jawaharlal Nehru (Madan 1994:1095). Madan claims to have been misunderstood, because "to draw attention to the limitations of the original ideology of secularism and its Indian version, and of their promoters, does not necessarily imply that one rejects the ideologies totally or the institutions that embody them" (Madan 1994: 1096). And in stark contrast with his earlier conclusion that he really has no "conclusions to offer, no solutions to suggest", Madan now feels that secularism should be "made into a national ethos", and in order to accomplish this, intellectuals "have to devise the most effective means of communication, carrying the people with them...." (Madan 1994: 1096). Such an exhortation gives the perception of a dramatic change in views.

However, despite such major concessions, Madan continues to attack straw persons while offering more of the same non-sociological and ahistorical interpretation of the issues at hand. Thus, without naming any scholars, for it would be impossible to find any who would fit his description, Madan attacks "intellec-tuals who proclaim that religion is not only a 'fake' but also necessarily evil, and therefore present secularism as a morally superior soteriology" (Madan 1994:1095). Who are these intellectuals who view religion as "necessarily evil"? Was secularism as a policy adopted in India because it was viewed as a "morally superior soteriology" or because of other practical exigencies that would confront any government vis-a-vis a religiously diverse nation? While engaging in the relatively easy and trendy task of criticising Nehru and his policies, Madan goes on to claim that he continues to be "sceptical about the easy confidence of secularists regarding the unproblematic adaptation [of secularism] " (Madan 1994:1069). Leaving aside the rhetoric of some politicians, it is hard to think of many intellectuals who expect the process of adaptation to any ideology or institution to be a smooth or trouble free process. Even to raise the issue of adaptation to an institution in a particular context would mean accepting the fact that secularism as a concept is indeed completely alien, having no basis whatsoever in the Indian cultural context. Madan of course, is not the first scholar to have expressed doubts about the adequacy of the practice of secularism for providing sufficient resources for the fight against communalism. Few scholars expect it to work as a formula that would erase all inter-communal tensions and conflicts away. Madan however, is one of the leading scholars who have set the trend of attributing the intensity and frequency of communal violence to the practice of secularism itself.

Andre Beteille has already discussed some of the problems associated with the recent ascendence of the anti-secularist impulse among some intellectuals in India. The same issue has also been discussed from a different angle in an earlier paper of mine (Baber 1996). It is Beteille's remarks about the curiously non-sociological conception of the relationship between religion and society that Madan has deployed that need further examination and scrutiny. In his recent writings on secularism, Madan treats religion and culture as neatly packaged, well defined, homogeneous and hermetically sealed entities. It is such a conception that makes it possible for him to identify, without any doubts or hesitation, "alien cultural" practices and ideologies like secularism which presumably do not resonate well with indigeneous, "traditional"

Indian realities. Madan's views are non-sociological not simply because he seems to have taken upon himself the task of identifiynig hermetically sealed cultural boundaries in order to distinguish between indigeneous Indian and alien cultural ideologies. Rather, he seems curiously unwilling to explore the dialectical interplay between religion and the changing social structures and institutions, whether in India or elsewhere. As pointed out by F.G. Bailey (1991) and Beteille (1994) among others, part of the reason for this curiously insular view of religion lies in Madan's easy acceptance of Dumontian doctrines of "holism" which makes it possible for him to assert that "religion is constitutive of society" in India.

It follows that one can safely ignore the mutually constitutive interplay between religion and society to set up a hierarchy of influences by arguing that for Indians, "the secular is regarded as encompassed by the religious" (Madan 1994:1096). In his earlier paper, after expounding at some length on the whole range of texts of various religions to be found in India, with the exception of Protestantism which apparently is at the root of the prob-lem, Madan wanted us to believe that he had firmly established that "the secular is encompassed by the sacred" (Madan 1987:753). Such a categorical but quite unwarranted assumption makes it possible for Madan to be convinced that the only way one can make sense of communalism in India is by undertaking detailed textual analyses of a wide assortment of religious doctrines, theological hair-splitting and the ferreting out of the implications of symbols and imageries for conflict at the societal level. It would seem that there is no need to engage in comparative historical analyses of the interconnections between changing social structures, religious ideas, institutions and practices. Thus, despite his admission that he "did perhaps overemphasise the holistic character of traditional religions" in his 1987 essay, Madan continues to focus exclusively on purported doctrinal differences between what he labels "traditional" religions and presumably non-traditional ones like Christianity to account for why a "Hindu or a Sikh, or a Muslim for that matter, would find it more difficult to make sense of the notion of privatisation of religion, than perhaps a Christian does" (Madan 1994:1096). Given such uncompromising culturalist assumptions, and provided one totally ignores the dramatic rise of Christian fundamentalism in various parts of the world, it is hardly surprising that Madan assumes that for people who subscribe to allegedly "non-traditional" religions, all action and behaviour is necessarily and completely dominated by a specific religious ethos. At the same it enables Madan to express surprise at the presumably "easy confidence of secularists regarding [the] unproblematic adaptation of secularism in the Indian context".

By way of explaining away the context in which his 1987 article was written, Madan ignores a whole tradition of serious and well grounded scholarship on the issue (Engineer, 1984; 1992; Thapar, Mukhia and Chandra, 1969; Thapar, 1989; Gupta, 1990; Gupta, Banerjee, Mohan and Navalakha, 1988; Chatterjee, 1992; Devalle, 1992; Helweg, 1987; van der Veer, 1987; 1988; 1992; Embree, 1990; Pandey, 1992; 1993; Basu 1995; Mazumdar 1995; Mehta and Shah, 1992;) to make the amazing claim that "there were not many intellectuals who....displayed any great unease about the recrudescence of religious fanaticism in the form of communalised politics or fundamentalist movements." Instead, he prefers to simplify and caricature the work of those scholars who have in fact examined the intricate connection between the struggle for political power, the changing economic situation and the mobilization of specific religious and ethnic identities to explain communal conflicts. He would really like all of us to believe that until he delivered his lecture which was published as an article, all secular intellectuals were simple minded individuals who could do little more than ask for "secularism and more secularism" (Madan 1994:1095). Such demands are of course highly problematic, because Madan obviously believes that this is a sure route to more communal conflagration as the theory and practice of secularism itself constitutes the major cause of communal strife. Beyond blunt assertions, Madan does not care to explain precisely how secularism has contributed to communal violence and the exact ways in which "religion itself could be a powerful resource in the struggle against religious extremism" (Madan 1994: 1095). Unless of course, one wants to follow the lead of professional politicians and continue to reiterate, in an abstract, ahistorical and non-sociological manner, the virtues presumably inherent in all religions. Indeed, in the wake of communal conflicts, what Madan seems to favour is the substitution of the secular intellectuals demand for "secularism and more secularism" by "religion and more religion".

In arguing that secularism "is impossible as a credo of life because the great majority of the people of South Asia are in their own eyes active adherents of some religious faith", Madan comes quite close to the resurrection of Orientalist and Indological fantasies about the essence of India. It is not at all clear precisely how adherence to some religious faith makes India so unique that the very presence of any secular institution is an affront to the religious sensibilities of people and automatically leads to communal conflicts. What sociological value is there in trying to characterize South Asians as "essentially religious" or even essentially secular when social life does not come in such neatly compartmentalized packages? However, Madan obviously believes that India constitutes the archetypical "religious" society, and little wonder that he is disdainful of the "arrogance" and "folly" of the misguided "dream of a minority [the secularists] which wants to shape the majority in its own image" (Madan 1987:748).

Madan however, wrote these lines a number of years ago. He now seems to hold the view that despite his intricate analysis of the *Dharamashastras* and the *Manusmriti* which he believes provides him with an accurate picture of all Indians as being completely impervious to secular ideas as understood in the "West", all is not lost, and secularism as a policy could be tried again, provided one keeps the uniquely religious character of Indian society in mind. His call for a project that would "clarify the notion of secularism in a context-sensitive manner" (Madan 1994:1096) would appear to be a major concession to the secularists. The caveat however, is that given that "religion is constitutive of Indian society", the adoption of secularism will take time and effort. Such a concession turns out to be hardly any concession at all, when one realizes that he defines secularism as "interreligious understanding". Such an understanding of secularism is indeed curious, even if one allows for the allegedly unique Indian context. Such an understanding of secularism and the process of secularisation are hardly to be found in the work of any sociologist writing on the issue (Lechner, 1991; Bellah, 1970; 1980). But then, these are "Western" scholars who can hardly be trusted for supplying concepts applicable to such non-Western and religious societies like India.

Even if one were to accept his contention that secularism needs to be redefined as "interreligious understanding" it is hard to envisage exactly how such a definition will be deployed for the formulation of public policy. Madan's call for deploying secularism in a "context sensitive manner" and the need for a kind of secularism that would "have to imply that those who profess no religion have a place in society equal to that of others, not higher or lower" does not help us in deciding how this principle might be translated into public policy. For example, what implications might such an understanding of secularism have in setting the curricula for sociology courses in universities? Or to use Beteille's example, the existence of universities as secular institutions does not in anyway imply the belittling of the religious beliefs of Indians, and it is not clear how secularism understood as "inter-religious tolerance" could be used to revamp existing universities. One could substitute the university with any major institution and raise the same question.

It is increasingly clear that the anti-secularist critics of Indian society, some of whom happen to be sociologists, have forsaken genuinely sociological analysis in favour of Indology where the actual behaviour of real living indivduals is ignored and Hindu religious texts are valourized to construct the essence of what Indian society is all about. Such sociologists continue to follow the instructions of Louis Dumont and David Pocock that one "should describe the common values and take care not to mix up facts of representation with the facts of behaviour" (Dumont and Pocock 1957). Of course, while launching their project for a "sociology of India", Dumont and Pocock equated Indian society with Hindu society and took their primary object of analysis to be a "system of ideas" rather than Indian society itself. Although anthropologists like F.G. Bailey promptly criticised the "strait-jacket they have designed for Indian sociology" because such an understanding came "near to defining sociology out of existence" and equated "Indian sociology with an analysis of the values of Hinduism" (Bailey 1959:88-91), the tradition continues to exercise an incredible hold on a dominant section of scholars claiming to analyze Indian society. The unease with the direction sociology of India has taken has been expressed by other sociologists like Imitiaz Ahmad (1976), Beteille (1974; 1991), Lardinois (1996) but the tradition continues to flourish, indulging without restraint in what A. N.

Whitehead termed "misplaced concreteness" or the confusion of concepts and texts for contextual reality.

In its latest incarnation, at the hands of some highly visible American scholars, the tradition has been pushed or perhaps "misplaced" to an entirely new level of "concreteness". Pushing a new brand of "Indian ethnosociology", the Chicago anthropo-logists McKim Marriott and his intellectual fellow-travellers seek nothing less than to provide alternatives to concepts that "have developed from thought about Western rather than Indian cultural realities". Hoping to exorcise "an alien ontology and an alien epistemology" from the discourse of social science in India, Mariott announces that while "class" and "status" might be "helpful concepts in the West, but [they] cannot separately or together define the transactional ways in which Hindu institutions order castes or persons." And while ostensibly attempting to construct an indigenous "Indian ethnosociology", Marriott, without any warning or any need to offer explanation, switches effortlessly from "Indian" to "Hindu" categories.

Although he does allude to "other possible Indian social sciences", and refers to the "windless Greco-Muslim humoral scheme reflected in the notions of Muslim farmers of Panjab and Sindh", the main objective of his work seems to be the construction of elaborate "Hindu constituent cubes", obtained, as he informs us through sophisticated "mathematical modelling" (1989: 32-33). Presumably other social scientists are free to construct analagous Muslim, Sikh, Parsee and "Other" constituent cubes and abstract conceptual schemes and the result is supposed to help us in getting rid of "alien ontology and alien epistemology" which hinder the understanding of Indian society. For the time being however, the papers that initially appeared in *Contributions to Indian Sociology* have been published as a separate volume with the appropriate title, *India Through Hindu Categories* (1990). Intellectual intentions notwithstanding and without any innuendo on my part, given the prevailing political atmosphere, the BJP and members of the Sangh Parivar and their supporters would no doubt be pleased with the title and the attempt to weed out "alien epistemology and ontology" which apparently do not fit Hindu realities! Not surprisingly, T.N. Madan contributes a preface to the volume which continues the tradition of Dumont and Pocock updated with an ethnosociological gloss. What if anything, such exercises contribute to the understanding of Indian society, whether past or present, is anybody's guess (Beteille, 1974).

Of course Madan and Marriot are not the only sociologists who have set aside their intellectual tools to provide ahistorical, incorrigibly culturalist accounts of the essence of Indian society while dismissing "western categories". Very much in line with the prevailing intellectual trends, sociologist Veena Das (1989) criticizes the "conception of a neutral, secular state" that "relies heavily upon the commonsense of Western social sciences". Alluding to Ayodhya by referring to "Hindus organizing into militant communities for the release of various sacred places that, given the cultural geography of India, are also sacred to the Muslims", she, like Madan and Ashis Nandy, dismisses the modernists and secularists because "the only answer modernists can offer...is to substitute national, sacred symbols for secular ones – and this is no answer at all". Worse still some of the solutions suggested by the simple minded secularists are unlikely to work as they do not take into account "the sentiments of both Hindus and Muslims about the sacred nature of these sites" (Das 1989: 46). However Das's attempt to accord such central importance to "sentiments" is quite out of line with surveys conducted by the news magazine *India Today* before the destruction of the mosque in Ayodhya.

More significantly, Ghanshyam Shah's survey, conducted after the Ayodhya demolition and in a city where communal violence was at its extreme in terms of brutality and barbarism, shows that such sentiments were accorded the lowest priority when compared to other issues (Shah 1994). Das's abstraction of ossified "sentiments" from a whole network of issues is quite unwarranted and such a formulation takes for granted a phenomenon that needs to be explained.

What one might ask is her solution to the problem? Predictably, the presumed traditions of the past are recommended as models worthy of emulation in the present. Das appears disheartened that "in the whole nationalist endeavour to transform Indian society, we have paid scant attention to the manner in which our past, in its essence, could be adapted for the future." While cautioning that "it is not frozen metaphors that we seek from our past, nor exotic myths and rituals that bear no relation to life whatsoever", she nevertheless urges us to "create forms of nationhood and state more responsive to our own historical experience" and to inculcate "the courage to experiment with our heritage" (Das 1989: 46). She however overestimates the power of intellectuals to influence events and in any case for the time being at least, it is the BJP ideologues and *kar sevaks* who have the resources and are indeed actively engaged in the "experiment with our heritage". What exactly, one might ask constitutes the raw material for such "courageous experiments with *our heritage*"? The essence of "*our heritage*" turns out to be the "principles of *varnadharma* and *purusartha*" and Das feels that an adequate response to the presumed modernist/secularist naivete lies in the charting out of "another notion of morality" based on "reflections on the theory of *purusartha*" or "four ends of life that a person might pursue.... *dharma*, *artha*, *kama*, and *moksa*" (p. 52). And while charting out an alternative notion of morality, Das urges us to "engage in a critique of the dominant monotheistic traditions of Islam and Christianity" because "rather than asking how Christianity or Islam may help us to discover montheistic trends within Hinduism, we may ask whether humankind has lost anything in its march towards monotheism" (p. 49).

Das's call for a change in values while ignoring the larger institutional transformations within India, as well as the wider forces of global capitalism is quite surprising, but well in line with received Indological wisdom. True, she does inject a note of caution by arguing that "no one can wish away the existence of markets or of modern nation-states", but seems confident enough that "secularists" and "modernists" are part of the problem, and the answers to problems of contemporary India are to found by delving into the past to search for appropriate values. Although Krishna (1992) has already expressed scepticism about such endeavours, one could extend his critique to ask whether all the Hindu textual concepts and categories invoked by Das do in fact really exhaust the entire range of "*our heritage*" and "*our historical experience*" in a multi-religious society. It is not clear exactly how the selective ferreting out of values from the past and their application to the present context will provide us with the "means to live together in diversity and make India the spiritual home of all those ideas that are under attack from fundamentalists and purists"? (Das 1989: 55). Das's voluntarism and idealism, springing from a valorization of textual constructs and her focus on values and spiritual ideas in isolation from institutions, social structures, political processes and the activities of real human beings bring us back to Dumont and Pocock's proposals "for a sociology of India". Even if all Indians could agree on the core values from the past, how exactly would this set of values, combined either with polytheism, monotheism or atheism help us to make sense of, let alone deal with the predicament of contemporary India? What insight does Das as a sociologist, not as a social or a spiritual philosopher, have to offer on the problem of communalism in India? To use F.G. Bailey's words, Das like Dumont and Pocock, indeed comes very "near to defining 'sociology' out of existence" (Bailey 1959: 91). While her views are very much in tune with the all too frequent dismissal of "modernity" and "secularism", it is intriguing that such ideas should come not from a social philosopher but a practising sociologist. But given the continued influence of Indology on some sociologists, such views should not surprise us, even as they constitute cause for concern.

However on the issue of secularism, neither Madan nor Das have gone quite as far as Ashis Nandy. Madan (1994: 1095) clearly perceives Nandy as a fellow-traveller and commends him for being one of the few intellectuals who "had dissented with this dominant discourse" of secularism. Of course Nandy, who does not claim to be a sociologist, has done more than simply express disagreement with those who have betrayed secular affinities. He has consistently heaped abuse on all those "decultured" "colonized" "rootless" Indians who conspire to spread such insidious ideologies as "rationality", "modernity", "secularism" and other associated evils. Nandy of course has been at it for quite some time, attributing all problems of contemporary India to the hidden but ubiquitous hand of colonialism, modernity, science and the "rootless" and "secularized" Indians. During the past few years he has increasingly taken it upon himself to give "voice to [the] ...semi-articulate protests...of marginalized Indians" (Nandy 1988:13). One of the means for achieving this goal has been to single out "secularists" and "modernists" who are either apparently quite lost about what is going on in India or worse, try to impose "Western" ideas on the people in an attempt to undermine the peace and tranquillity that was presumably the natural state of affairs in "traditional", pre-colonial India.

Coinciding with the increasing "intolerance" of secular ideas and institutions, Nandy has let loose a volley of abuse at secularists, labelling them variously as "intellectually crippled and morally flawed", "senile", "seduced and brainwashed", "anaemic" and colonized by an "imperialism of categories" (Nandy 1992). Indeed, following his predictable pattern of viewing the world through rigid dichotomies of East/West, Orient/Occident, tradition/modernity, sacred/secular, "White Man/WOG" (his terms!), Nandy has even argued that secularism is nothing less than a "Western and colonial concept...introduced into Indian public life...to subvert and discredit" Indian society. It turns out that secular intellectuals in trying to impose the "western" concept of secularism on a traditional society like India, have "taken over the white man's burden in this part of the world...[and] see it as their bounden duty to educate and modernize the citizens of this part of the world..." (Nandy 1992: 28). Nandy's abstract formula is indeed a handy if intellectually lazy device for explaining almost anything, without having to examine the specificity of any process. And indeed he has resorted to the "blame it on colonialism, science and modernity" formula quite frequently over the past twenty years. Not surprisingly, he even invoked these factors to explain the case of *sati* in 1987! As Nandy argued in the now infamous article, Roop Kanwar was apparently engaged in a "desperate attempt to retain through *sati* something of the religious world-view in an increasingly desacralized, secular world" (Nandy 1987b). After all, forced to live in a public sphere controlled by "colonized", "secularized", "rootless" and "decultured" individuals, Roop Kanwar apparently decided to take the step because at least the practice of *sati* "reaffirms, even if in a bizarre, violent and perverted fashion, respect for self-sacrifice in a culture in which increasingly there is no scope or legitimacy for self-sacrifice" (Nandy 1987b). The issue of why women once again have to bear the burden of upholding tradition and self-sacrifice is not raised and the origins of such a desacralized and secular culture of course lie in modernity introduced into India through the agency of colonialism. As Aijaz Ahmad (1992: 196-7) has aptly remarked, "colonialism is now held responsible not only for its own cruelties but, conveniently enough for ours too". If one were to believe Nandy, everything that has ever happened or will happen in contemporary India is partly either due to the hidden hand of colonialism or the actions of the "children of Macaulay". Contemporary Indians are presumably devoid of any agency.

What about the oft-repeated claim that "secularism was introduced in a big way in the early decades of the century...to subvert and discredit the traditional concepts of inter-religious tolerance that had allowed the thousands of communities living in the subcontinent to co-survive in neighbourliness"? (Nandy 1992: 28). He is indeed ignoring plenty of historical evidence to conjure up a "mythography" of a tranquil, non-violent pre-colonial Indian past. Such formulations are well in line with his repeated rejection of "objective" history and the promotion of "mytho-graphies". But for those who are not quite convinced that there are no shades of grey between "objective" history and "mytho-graphy", such stories are not quite convincing. Indeed even Nandy acknowledges the existence of occasional strife and violence in pre-colonial times, but explains it away by arguing "such violence never involved large aggregates such as the Hindus or the Muslims" as no one has produced an iota of convincing empirical evidence to show that such conflicts existed on a large scale and involved religious communities *as they are presently defined....*" (my emphasis).

Of course, by asking others to produce evidence of pre-colonial conflicts involving "religious communities *as they are presently defined*" Nandy is sending them on a fool's errand (Bayly, 1985; Talbot, 1995). One need not accept the colonialist historiography on the issue of communal conflicts to appreciate the problems with Nandy's mode of reasoning. Of course, "reason" or "rationality" is not exactly in fashion these days. Indeed the profound ambivalence towards instrumental rationality and certain aspects of modernity expressed by Max Weber and some thinkers of the Frankfurt School has now been replaced by an all too glib dismissal of all forms of modernity and rationality. Indeed when it comes to rationality and modernism, Nandy is not only throwing out the proverbial baby with the bathwater, but he seems to have taken it upon himself to wreck all bath-tubs in sight.

Nandy is so enthralled and fascinated with his own conceptual abstractions and the clever turn of the phrase that any critique of his work only encourages him. What is curious however is that his current blanket denunciation of "rationality", "modernity", "science" and "secularism" is quite at odds with his earlier ideas and research when he indeed had, to use his words, "taken over the white man's burden". In the seventies, Nandy was very actively involved in conducting research which was completely informed by the worst aspects of "modernization theory". Indeed not only was he not averse to scientistic research techniques, but was actively measuring the level of "modernity" and the infamous "need for Achievment" or "n-Ach" among the residents of Howrah. Thus in contrast to his recent dismissal of "objective" historiography and the demand for its replacement by "mythographies", Nandy in the 1970's was measuring "modernity" on the "OM and RM scale", and was assigning "beta weights" to each measure of "N-Achievment" in order to ascertain the "correlates and predictors of entrepreneural competence" among different castes (Owens and Nandy 1977: 166). After taking careful measure of "entrepreneur's innovativeness by averaging the ratings for the two independent observers on a two-point scale", Nandy and his co-researcher subjected the results to "regression analysis". This enabled them to reach the conclusion that "though the intercaste difference in the correlation between entrepreneurship and n-Achievment is not significant, the near zero beta weight of n-Achievment among the Mahisyas suggests that in their less modern but more entrepreneurial subculture, the need does not directly contribute to entrepreneurship." While cautioning that "without a nonrecursive path analysis one cannot speak the language of causal modelling", Nandy succeeded in establishing that "even when the effects of all other variables are removed, the beta weight for n-Achievement remains a redoubt-able .28 – the highest among all the variables in the equation for the upper castes" (Owens and Nandy 1977: 160-61).

In marked contrast to his recent discovery of idealized constructs like "traditional values", Nandy had earlier contended that "with Independence, education, and so on India is moving towards a mass culture in which the distinctiveness of caste groups is breaking down" (Owens and Nandy 1977:17). Based on his accurate measurement of "n-Ach", Nandy had reasoned that such a situation will come about because "when formerly low-placed groups become involved in secondary industrialization the result is a wide transformation of the society in accordance with more egalitarian values". In line with the main thrust of modernization theory, historical specificities were ignored and Nandy could confidently predict that such results were to be expected "wherever secondary industrialization occurs" (Owens and Nandy 1977: 196-97).

The discussion above is not meant to question Nandy's research findings from the seventies. Such an exercise would be redundant. In view of the complexities of the development process and the emergence of a number of perspectives to make sense of these processes, criticizing modernization theory at this stage would be worse than flogging the proverbial dead horse. The same goes for McLelland's "n-Ach" theory and all the attempts to come up with abstract measures of "modernity". What is remarkable of course is the complete inversion of Nandy's view: from the total acceptance of modernization theory to the total dismissal of any redeeming features of "modernity", "secularism" and "rationality". There seems to be little room for comprehending the many ambiguities and various facets of modernities, secularisms and rationalities. Nandy's constant demand for a return to the alleged tranquility and harmony of "traditional" India might constitute a plausible though unworkable social philosophy, but it betrays limited understanding of the development and transformation of social institutions and ideologies over time. The irony of Nandy's obsession with colonialism, the "West" and the "imperialism of categories" is that his project grants too much power to the very ideas and institutions that he wants to challenge. And the power of the "imperialism of categories" is nowhere more evident than in Nandy's construction of neat binary categories and smug dismissal of all aspects of modernity. The philosopher Akeel Bilgrami's (1993: 293) reference to the "neurotic obsession with the Western and colonial determination of their present condition" and his remark that "it will prove a final victory for imperialism that after all the other humiliations it has visited..., it lingered in our psyches in the form of genuine self-understanding to make self-criticism and free, unreactive agency impossible", although made in a quite different context, is not irrelevant for the kind of project Ashis Nandy and his followers have embarked upon.

One of the unintended but unfortunate consequences of the recent unrelenting intellectual onslaught on "secularism" and the yearning for simpler, traditional, uncorrupted past has been the unwitting support to the dominant BJP/RSS/VHP discourse which such discussions have provided. If Ashis Nandy contends that "secularism" supported by "modernized" "rootless" "senile" and "secular" intellectuals began corrupting the purity of "traditional" India during the colonial period, the BJP/RSS/VHP ideologue agrees with the essential outline of this argument, disagreeing only with the periodization. The colonial period is replaced by the "Muslim rule", but the argument and reasoning, although geared towards very different ends, remains pretty much the same. The same goes for Madan and Nandy's favourite quote from Gandhi: "those who say religion has nothing to do with politics do not know what religion means", a quote that is wrenched out of its context and presented as transhistorical truth. It is hardly surprising that the BJP flaunted the same quote from Gandhi to legitimize its view on the relationship between religion and politics at its national conference held in Bangalore. At the same time, some anti-secularist intellectuals try to distinguish between what they perceive to be "good" and "bad" religion. This is evident in the oft-repeated distinction between "religion as ideology" and "religion as faith" (Sethi 1992). Apparently parties like the BJP are mobilizing "religion as ideology" to attain their political goals, whereas Nandy, Madan and others would presumably like to promote "religion as faith". The problem of course is that the presumed distinction between "religion as ideology" and "religion as faith" is not very convincing. Indeed the narrow focus on religion per se as constituting the main cause of communal problems or the idea that somehow the restoration of the correct religious values (religion as faith!) which are apparently being suppressed by forces of "statism" will resolve most of the problems reflects an unwarranted confidence in the power of autonomous "values" and ideologies. Such formulations also betray a high degree of sociological naivete about the realationship between ideas, interests, agency and social structure.

Overall, the sustained intellectual attack on secularism and the repeated attempts to identify "alien", "Western" cultural influences that have presumably contaminated the purity of indigenous institutions betrays a very ahistorical and non-sociological understanding of the constitution of cultures and institutions. Such writings have contributed precious little toward understanding the current communal problem in India. On the contrary, they have indeed resonated rather well with the current Hindutva ideology. Critics of secularism, especially those who claim to reject Hindutva ideology and complain that they being unfairly labeled as "communalists" will have to do better than simply confess that they have "no solutions to offer". It would of course be naive on my part to expect clear cut practical solutions, but the anti-secularist intellectuals should at least attempt to provide some theoretical clues as to exactly how the universities, banks, the economy, hospitals, the judiciary, the civil service, the transportation system etc. should be re-organized on non-secular, religious lines to take into account the fact of "god as creator and protector, and the sustainer of human societies" (Srinivas cited in Beteille 1994: 460). Or exactly how the major institutions in India should be revamped to accomodate the demand that "those who profess no religion have a place in society equal to that of others, not higher or lower" (Madan 1987: 758). At the very least one could expect some theoretical clues about the specific ways in which restoration of values from the past would contribute to communal harmony under the radically different institutional context of the present. However tempting the lore and lure of an invented past with its presumed traditions and values as depicted in classical texts might be, the anti-secularist intellectuals might do well to reflect on the dramatically changed and changing economic, social and political context of the present. As Beteille has reminded us, "no civilization has ever prospered either by holding on to every idea and institution inherited from the past or by completely insulating itself from all that is exogenous" (Beteille 1994: 560). Indeed given the continuous exchange and transformation of ideas and institutions, one could go further than Beteille to question the reification of clear-cut categories of "alien" and "indigenous" that Madan and others valorize. This is of course not to argue that the current trend of globalization will necessarily lead to cultural and institutional homogenization. Indeed distinctive institutions and cultural patterns will continue to be reconstituted, but surely it is hardly possible to seal off cultures and institutions from each other. In any case India was hardly ever sealed off from other cultures and institutions even in the distant past. Unless one wants to accept the current BJP/RSS/VHP line that prior to the "Muslim rule", India, conceived of as a perfectly constituted entity from "time immemorial", was never exposed to any "alien" influences! But even the most determined cultural purist and segregationist who believes that secularism is an "alien" ideology might do well to reflect on Beteille's point that "the test of an idea or an institution should be its capacity to meet our present needs and not its provence....geography can never be a decisive test of the social value of an idea or an institution" (Beteille 1994:560).

One of the unfortunate aspects of the debate on secularism has been the excessively narrow focus on religion, religious values and the projects and politics of communal parties alone. As

Ashwini K. Ray (1993) and other scholars have argued, it is about time that social scientists located communal and ethnic conflict within the larger socio-economic and political transformations in India and globally. There is no doubt that despite certain specific characteristics, communal conflicts in India share certain generic features with ethnic, racial and fascist types of conflicts where religion does not appear to be directly implicated. More often than not, religious affilitation in India serves as a marker of group identity. If such an assumption is granted, it makes little sociological sense to focus on religious factors alone while analyzing communal conflicts. Such analyses and critiques of the hyper-valorization of "tradition" evident in the writings of Aijaz Ahmad (1993a; 1993b) Vanaik (1997), Dipankar Gupta (1988; 1990), Asghar Ali Engineer (1984; 1990), Roger and Patricia Jeffery (1994), Hansen (1996), Tambiah (1996), van der Veer (1995), Jaffrelot (1996), Basu (1995), Kurien (1994), Basu and Subra-maniam (1996), Bilgrami (1994), Nussbaum (2002; 2003) and others will hopefully provide the route for moving out of the endless Indological, culturological and non-sociological dissection of religious texts, doctrines, world-views and cosmologies that are presumed to encompass and dominate all aspects of the lives of all humans at all times. There are ample signs of the decline of the dominance of non-sociological, non-reflexive fluff that has proliferated for quite some time.

As for Ashis Nandy's smug confidence that almost everything that happens in contemporary India can be attributed either to the hidden hand of colonialism or the insidious machinations of "modern" "decultured", "senile", "rootless", "anaemic academic secularists", one can only wonder if there are any limits to what Marx called "theoretical bubble-blowing" and E.P. Thompson, barely a few months before his death, referred to as the "destructive theoreticism of some intellectuals" (Thompson 1992). While restrospective constructions of harmonious, peaceful pre-colonial pasts might be morally comforting and constitute good "mythographies", they are poor substitutes for objective (if such an outdated term can be used) historical and sociological analysis. The real problems associated with objectivity in the social sciences nothwithstanding, to reject "objective" historiography and sociological analysis in favour of "mythographies" is to concede the terms of debate to the Sangh Parivar activists who are better placed not just to construct but also to enforce their own "mythographies".

HINDUTVA AND THE MAINSTREAMING OF BIGOTRY

India cannot be assumed today to be a unitarian and homogeneous nation, but on the contrary there are two nations in the main; the Hindus and the Muslims... There are two antagonistic nations living side by side in India. (Savarkar, 1937)

It is extremely difficult to appreciate why our Hindu friends fail to understand the real nature of Islam and Hinduism. They are not religions in the strict sense of the word, but are, in fact, different and distinct social orders, and it is a dream that the Hindus and Muslims can ever evolve a common nationality. (Jinnah, 1940)

The Emergence of Secular Nationalism and the Decline of Religious Authority

The dramatic rise of "religious nationalism" in various regions of the world appears to be a phenomenon that seems to contradict the fundamental assumptions of the Enlightenment. It is of course true that the leading Enlightenment thinkers of the eighteenth century were not critical of religion per se. Rather, they were critical of clerical authority of their times, and indeed it was Rousseau who coined the term "civil religion" to characterize the existence of belief systems that pervaded the civil society of eighteenth century France (Zeitlin, 1994). Despite the carving out of a space for such generalized beliefs such as the existence of God etc., the relationship between political and religious authority was fundamentally restructured in late eighteenth century Europe.

As many social historians have convincingly argued, prior to the conflict between political and religious authority, the medieval church possessed many of the attributes that are now associated with the state (Strayer, 1971). In retrospect, such a situation is not surprising in view of the fact that in medieval Europe, political institutions relied on religion to legitimize their authority. The gradual replacement of religious political institutions by secular ones constitutes one of the distinctive features of modernity. With the emergence of the modern nation-state, secular nationalism appeared as the logical and indeed ideological ally to take over the role of religion as the cement that glued disparate communities to the political structures. The gradual replacement of religion by secular nationalism was possible only within the context of a number of dramatic structural changes in the late eighteenth and nineteenth centuries that expanded the "administrative reach" (Giddens, 1985) of the state apparatus. These changes included the expansion of transportation and communication networks, the growth of capitalism and markets, mass education, the creation and standardization of national languages etc. (Giddens 1985; Kiernan, 1988). Such radical transformations affected the organization as well as what one might call the "moral reach" (Juergensmeyer 1995) of some religious institutions. Protestant denominations and less powerful versions of Roman Catholicism jostled with each other to usurp the authority of the established church. The long and drawn out process of the replacement of religion by secular nationalism as the major ideological force was accelerated and accompanied by the dramatic expansion of the various organizational and ideological components of the modern nation-state. Much later, this "moral reach" of religious authority sought to expand in the form of electronic churches, tele-evangelism and more recently, the on-line construction of transnational religious and communal identities via the internet (Rai, 1995).

Drawing upon the work of Mark Juergensmeyer (1995; 1996) it can be argued that one of the distinctive features of the modern period is the ability of the secular state to deny the right of religious authorities to be the ultimate moral arbiters. Although Max Weber argued that the defining characteristic of the state is its claim of monopoly over the legitimate use of violence within a specific territory (Weber, 1958:78), it should be kept in mind that this monopoly was not always easy to enforce. The claims to such a monopoly followed on the heels of intense rivalry and competition between the church and the emerging nation-state. The social historian Ainslie Embree (1990:2) describes the era as one in which "nationalism and religion, which reinforced each other in the conflicts of the seventeenth century were replaced by nationalism alone." However, it is clear that the contemporary resurgence of conflicts apparently fueled by religion indicates that the issue in favor of a secular nation-state is far from settled. The rise of what Juergensmeyer (1995) calls "the new religious state", is indeed a fact in Iran, Sudan and parts of Afghanistan. A similar trend can be discerned in Algeria, India and of course Israel, where Rabin was assassinated apparently on orders from God. In the United States, the influence of evangelists of various sorts on domestic and foreign policies is quite evident too.

At one level, the resurgence of "religious nationalism" in conflict with "secular nationalism" should not come as a surprise since both can be conceived of as ideologies of order and share a number of distinctive characteristics. Both deal with the world around them as a coherent, manageable system; both claim to articulate some deeper meaning beneath the mundane daily grind that constitutes life; both claim to provide identity for their followers and demand various degrees of loyalty in return; finally, both seek to provide the authority that gives social and political order a reason for being (Juergensmeyer, 1995:380). As the oft-quoted term "imagined communities" coined by Benedict Anderson (1983) implies, religion and nationalism both participate in the constitution of such communities and both seek to command communal loyalties and to transform power into authority. As for further similarities between religious and secular nationalism, Alexis de Tocqueville's comment that the French Revolution had "many aspects of a religious revolution" and his description of secular nationalism as the "strange religion" that had "overrun the whole world with its apostles, militants, and martyrs" (Tocqueville, 1955:11-13). Through the agency of colonial expansion and the proliferation of various ideologies, the "secular missionaries" were to spread the new gospel to many parts of the world during the nineteenth century. If the pre-modern period exhibited a symbiotic albeit uneasy co-existence of religious and state authority, and the modern period was characterized by the emergence of secular nationalism as the alternative to religion as the legitimating ideology for the state, late modernity can be seen to have brought religious and secular nationalisms into conflict and competition with each other (Juergensmeyer, 1995). Whether an increasing number of societies are headed towards the "new religious state" or not is hard to say, but there is no doubt that one of the contradictions of modernity is the dramatic rise of religious nationalism in the contemporary world. The section below examines deploys the framework discussed above to examine the situation in contemporary India.

Colonialism, Religious Nationalism and the Construction of Imagined Communities in India

Although a sense of belonging to specific communities existed in pre-colonial India, the relative stabilization of specifically Hindu and Muslim communal identities was mainly a consequence of colonial rule. This does not mean that the colonial policy of "divide and rule" conjured up communal identities from scratch or that the hidden hand of colonial history should be treated as the master explanatory device for interpreting communal conflicts in contemporary India. To adopt such an argument would amount to the replication of Orientalist fantasies that concede little by way of agency to Indians. As Aijaz Ahmad (1992:196-7) has perceptively observed, "colonialism is now being held responsible not only for its own cruelties, but conveniently enough, for ours too." However, in whatever inchoate forms communities may have existed in pre-colonial India, the process of institutionalizing specific communities was intimately associated with the administrative imperatives of the colonial state. In broad sociological terms, such administrative imperatives were part and parcel of what Max Weber called the rationalization process. The emerging colonial state, confronted with the task of governing a vast population and territory had to devise mechanisms for the legitimation of its rule as well as to simplify what it claimed to be an indecipherable complexity of castes and communities having specific characteristics and propensities.

Without intending to argue that religious communities were simply a colonialist invention, one can agree with the findings of many historians who have pointed out that the division of the Indian population into discrete religious communities constituted an integral strategy of colonial practice (Pandey, 1990; van der Veer, 1994). This is clearly evident in many aspects of colonial administration, but especially so in the sphere of legal institutions and practices. In their attempt to decode, standardise and apply "indigenous" law, the British made a clear-cut distinction between "Hindu" and "Muhammedan" law. The census further codified and institutionalised these distinctions in terms of a Hindu "majority" and a Muslim "minority" that became the basis of electoral, representative politics. The extensive reliance on religious specialists for interpreting, constructing, and codifying indigenous laws as represented by Nathaniel Halhed's *Code of Gentoo Laws* (1776) amongst other texts, played a substantial role in the process of constituting relatively homogenous religious communities from very diverse strands. A majority of institutions that developed after this period incorporated the assumption of relatively homogenous Hindu and Muslim communities.

Although many practices of the colonial rulers constituted part and parcel of the process of rationalisation of administrative institutions and colonial state formation, they simultaneously contributed to the relative stability of self-perceptions and constitution of specific Indian communities. Thus the "Orientalist" faction of colonial administrators represented by William Jones, Natahaniel Halhed, Prinsep, etc., constructed India as an ancient Hindu civilization in which Brahmanical authority was and had always been paramount. While emphasizing the common Indo-European roots of Western and Hindu civilization, the same narrative also deployed a version of Indian history whose key motif and indeed recurring theme was the decline of Hindu civilization under "Muslim" rule. In this narrative that was to soon to become the hegemonic discourse, the colonial administrators saw themselves as the protectors and custodians of their Hindu subjects against the "oriental despotism" of Muslims. The discourse of "oriental despotism" was of course firmly established in general European intellectual history from Aristotle to Montesquieu and Hegel (Zeitlin 1994). As such, it was readily available as an ideological resource and was deployed effectively, particularly during the battles of the

East India Company against Mysore's Hyder Ali and Tipu Sultan. However, the deployment of the discourse of "oriental despotism" by the colonial authorities was not restricted to the late eighteenth century. In general, Islam in India was regarded as culturally identical to and part and parcel of the Islamic civilization centering on the Middle East. The Hindus on the other hand were represented as the true natives of India, whose ancient, pre-Islamic civilization was worthy of attention but whose present condition had been rendered deplorable as a consequence of "Muslim" rule. Colonial rule was considered to be the prime agency through which the pre-Islamic grandeur of authentic, Hindu India could be restored to its former glory (van der Veer, 1994:20). A recurring master narrative deployed to legitimate colonial rule revolved around the idea that the British constituted an enlightened "race" who under the conditions had no choice but to lead the Indian people out of the problematic situation they were in. The argument that was frequently made was that the British in colonial India represented a secular Christian nation who had a rational interest in modernizing a society torn apart by sectarian conflict and chaos.

These discourses provided support for and were constitutive of a number of administrative and judicial institutions. More significantly, they also contributed in large measure to the "imagined communities" (Anderson, 1983) of Hindus and Muslims that were and continue to be internally divided and extremely heterogeneous (E. Mann, 1992). Needless to add, the leaders and orchestrators of such imagined communities did not passively accept colonial definitions and initiatives. Rather, they were active agents who mobilized such ideas and formulations in pursuit of specific interests and goals that were quite often at variance with colonial imperatives and objectives. At the risk of simplifying complex historical, social and political configurations, it can be argued that competing narratives deployed by the purported elites of a number of such imagined communities, in conjunction with specific structural contexts, have played a significant role in the precipitation of communal conflicts in contemporary India. Thus, the Orientalist discourse of the decline of Indian civilization as a consequence of "Muslim" rule was internalized and deployed by a number of Hindu reformers like Dayananda, Vivekananda and others who called for a revitalization and homogenization of their community (Chatterjee, 1986). Despite their explicit reliance on and active deployment of colonialist constructions of Indian history, they identified the "West" and their British representatives as part of the problem, and called for a nationalist struggle based on Hindu religious idioms. Simultaneously, Muslim reformers, like Syed Ahmad Khan, the founder of Aligarh Muslim University and the theologians associated with the religious institution in Deoband, although from a very different perspective, sought to revitalize what they perceived to be a once dominant but now vanquished and decaying Islamic commu-nity. The narrative of a Muslim community in decline was and continues to be a mythical construction precisely because it was a relatively small Muslim elite and not Muslims in general who lost power in the eighteenth century. Indeed, throughout the so-called "Muslim" rule, the vast majority of the Muslim population did not share any more in the control of the state apparatus or wealth than the Hindus. Nevertheless, Hindus as well as Muslims were able to effectively draw upon and deploy Orientalist discourses, albeit for different ends (van der Veer, 1994: 21). To argue that such discourses are mythical constructions is obviously not to contend that they are "false". Rather, such discourses served to define reality in specific ways at particular structural and historical conjunctures and provided the resources and basis for political action, both on behalf of such "communities" as well as against them by other "communities".

The echo of colonialist narratives and policies is nowhere more evident than in the writings of those who either took it upon themselves or were pushed into that role by the colonial authorities to represent Hindu and Muslim communities. This tradition begins in the nineteenth century, and continues in one form or the other in contemporary India, although it has been adapted and transformed, depending on specific contextual factors. Witness the modernist Muslim reformer, Sir Syed Ahmad Khan criticizing the Indian National Congress in 1888:

> The aims and objects of the Indian National Congress are based upon an ignorance of history and present-day realities; they do not take into consideration that India is inhabited by different nationalities; they presuppose that the Muslims, the Marathas, the Bengalis, the Madrasis, and the Pesawaris can all be treated alike and all of them belong to the same nation. The Congress thinks that they profess the same religion, that they speak the same language, that their way of life and customs are the same.... I consider the experiment which the Indian National Congress wants to make fraught with dangers and suffering for all the nationalities of India, especially of the Muslims (Hay, 1988: 192).

Contrary to popular perceptions, at this stage, Sir Syed was not even close to being the main spokesman for Indian Muslims, although he represented the incipient, modernist "separatist" school. The other more orthodox and conservative school associated with the theological institutions at Deoband, was in fact supportive of the Congress movement and was "accomo-dationist" rather than "separatist". In fact this "orthodox" Muslim faction was consistently against partition on religious lines.

The Hindu counterparts to Sir Syed's conception of the irreconcilable differences between various communities in pre-partition India were Aurobindo Ghose, Bankim Chatterjee, Tilak, Lajpat Rai, Malaviya, V.D. Savarkar and others who with varying degrees and emphases were explicit in their Hindu religious imagery and fiery rhetoric. Writing in 1937 in a famous tract titled *Hindutva* that continues to be the prime source of inspiration for the present day Bhartiya Janata Party, V. D. Savarkar argued:

> India cannot be assumed today to be a unitarian and homo-geneous nation, but on the contrary there are two nations in the main; the Hindus and the Muslims... There are two antagonistic nations living side by side in India (Larson, 1995:188).

Such views were not uncommon within the Congress party in the early stages and these perceptions were not inconsequential in driving away the Muslim supporters of the nationalist movement, who began to perceive the Congress as a cover for Hindu hegemony. As some scholars like Gerald Larson (1995) have pointed out, Jinnah, the architect of Pakistan, in issuing the call for partition in March 1940 echoed Savarkar's views:

> It is extremely difficult to appreciate why our Hindu friends fail to understand the real nature of Islam and Hinduism. They are not religions in the strict sense of the word, but are, in fact, different and distinct social orders, and it is a dream that the Hindus and Muslims can ever evolve a common nationality.... The Hindus and Muslims belong to two different religious philosophies, social customs, literatures. They neither intermarry nor interdine together and, indeed, they belong to two different civilizations which are based mainly on conflicting ideas and conceptions (Jinnah quoted in Larson, 1995:189).

Guru Golwalkar, the leader of RSS, the quasi-fascist organization that continues to be an active ally of the ruling Bhartiya Janata Party, conceived of the Hindus and Muslims as separate "races" and drew attention to Hitler's Germany as a possible model for India. In a famous tract titled *We, Our Nationhood Defined* (1943), Golwalkar argued:

> The other nation most in the eye of the world today is Germany. This nation affords a very striking example. German race pride

> has now become the topic of the day. To keep up the purity of the Race and its culture, Germany shocked the world by her purging the country of the semitic Races - the Jews. Race pride at its highest has been manifested here. Germany has also shown how well nigh impossible it is for Races and cultures, having differences going to the root, to be assimilated into one united whole, a good lesson for us in Hindusthan to learn and profit by (Golwalkar, 1944:36-37).

Picking up the Orientalist discourse of Muslims as "foreigners", and imbuing them with a distinctive "racial" identity, Golwalkar offered a way out for them:

> Emigrants have to get themselves naturally assimilated in the principal mass of population, the national Race, by adopting its culture and language and sharing in its aspirations, by losing all consequences of their separate existence, forgetting their foreign origin.....That is the only logical and correct solution....in one word, they must cease to be foreigners, or may stay in the country, wholly subordinated to the Hindu nation, claiming nothing, not even citizen's rights (Golwalkar, 1944:49).

Extremist rhetoric from both sides actively contributed to the consolidation of a sense of homogeneous and "racial" communal identity. Although the Hindu extremists were eventually to lose their influence within the Congress Party (others were associated with non-Congress organizations like the Hindu Mahasabha, the Arya Samaj etc.), certain fundamental institutional changes ushered in by the colonial government provided further support to the emergent Hindu and Muslim "community". These changes included the partition of Bengal on religious lines by Lord Curzon in 1905 (rescinded in 1911-12) and the numerous electoral reforms beginning with the Morley-Minto Reforms of 1909 that provided for separate electorates for Muslims, Sikhs, Anglo-Indians, Indian Christians and the Scheduled Castes. It is not quite accurate to argue that these electoral reforms directly precipitated modern communalism and the creation of Pakistan. However, there is no doubt that this continual interplay of agency and structure, religious communities, orientalist ideologies, the colonial state and other institutions, mutually constituted each other and have contributed to the contemporary problems at hand.

The Mobilization of Memory and Communal Conflicts in Contemporary India

It is arguable that the past has no real purchase on communal conflicts in contemporary India. It is of course true that communal conflicts in contemporary India have their own dynamics, rooted in the ongoing quest for political power, the changing nature of the relationship between the central and the provincial governments and the response of the traditional elites to their ongoing decline as a consequence of structural changes etc. (Basu and Kohli 1997; Kohli 1997; Basu, 1997; Gupta 1990). However, it would be a mistake to ignore the role of the constant mobilization and attempts to re-configure fragments of social memory for deployment in the present. The attempt to construct and codify the periodization of Indian history as Hindu, Muslim and British; the institutionalization of the memory of the horrors of the bloodshed that ensued partition; the largely successful erasure from social memory that the partition was not by any means a generalized "Muslim" demand but the demand of a specific political party; the erasure from memory of the fact that separatism was also a strong movement amongst the Indian Tamils for quite a few decades (Irschick, 1969; Barnett, 1976), and continues to be so in certain "Hindu" provinces like Manipur in Northeast India have all contributed to the consolidation of imagined Hindu and Muslim communities as irreconcilable yet inextricably connected elements of the "self" and the "other".

Indeed some Hindu chauvinist ideologues contend that

the root cause of communal conflict is a false representation of what is labelled as the "Muslim" period of Indian history. Much of their ire is directed towards the social historians associated with the Jawaharlal Nehru University and who offer a Marxist or rather structural and contextualist interpretation of medieval India. The Hindu parties and ideologues consider interpretations that would be accepted as standard sociological analysis and historiography as a deliberate, ideologically motivated, secu-larized, sanitized version of history that seeks to cover up a period that led to the constant and unrelenting subjugation of all the Hindus by all the Muslims. Any attempt to contextualize the actions of specific regimes from the so-called "Muslim" period is interpreted as nothing more than an apology for the past. A structural and political explanation of the basis of conflict between "Muslim" rulers and their subjects is also dismissed as a deliberate ploy designed to rob an imagined "Hindu community" of their right to create a Hindu theocratic state in the post-colonial era. As mentioned earlier, much of this selective retention of memory derives from patently orientalist and colonialist constructions, and the would be leaders of both imagined communities of Hindus and Muslims dip into and impart their own spin for making sense (or perhaps nonsense) of and dealing with present realities.

Lest it appear that this paper has offered an idealistic interpretation of the constitution of communities and communal conflict in contemporary India, it should be made clear that the political economy of communalism is no less important and it is hardly a question of prioritizing one over the other. Indeed as mentioned earlier, access to political and economic power has been the driving force behind communal conflicts in India, as in fact is the case in other parts of the world too. The partition, the conflict in Punjab, as well as the recurring communal conflicts in India have all been accurately interpreted by using a political economy perspective (Engineer 1984; Gupta 1990). The intention of this paper is not to argue, as indeed some writers have suggested, that religion, social memory or even the discipline of history (Sheldon Pollock, 1993) are primarily responsible for precipitating communal violence in India. Quite in contrast to such formulations, the point of this paper is that religion, memory and history are always available in one form or the other for mobilization by specific communities, both for constructing their communities and for staking a claim to the present. Whether such symbolic resources will actually be mobilized or not, will of course depend on particular historical, political and economic conjunctures.

To come back to the issue of the emerging conflict and competition between religious and secular nationalism, it is unlikely that the former will disappear as predominantly agrarian societies modernize and are incorporated within the circuits of global capitalism. The assumption that religious nationalists are trying to turn the clock back is problematic because they are attempting nothing of that sort. On the contrary, as many scholars have pointed out, they are creatures of modernity, trying to stake a claim for the future (Embree 1990). Perhaps this phenomenon can be better understood by considering Juergensmeyer's (1995:388) distinction between "modernity" and "modernism". If "modernity" can be broadly understood as the acceptance of bureaucratic forms of organization and the acquisition of new technology and "modernism" as the ideology of individualism and a relativist view of moral values, religious nationalists can be considered modern, without being modernists. The upsurge of religious nationalism can be seen as strengthening a particular definition of national identities, and as such this phenomenon is not incompatible with modernity.

In the case of India, the postcolonial state was pre-dominantly secular in its orientation, although it was a particular and peculiar definition of secularism that did not imply a strict separation between religion and public policies. Rather the whole political process consisted of making concession to and accommodating a wide variety of religious demands and pressures from *all* religious communities. Secularism in the Indian context was defined as "equal respect for all religions" rather than equal indifference to all religions in the sphere of public policy. Contrary to the dominant interpretations offered by scholars like T. N. Madan (1987) Veena Das (1989), Ashis Nandy (1985) etc. who argue that the very policy of aggressive secularism has contributed to communal violence, it can be argued that the extremely ambiguous relationship between the state and religion has led to the escalation of pressures for further concessions from all religious groups. In India, members from religious political parties have been elected to the national and state assemblies, religious schools have been affiliated with the state and temples, mosques, churches and gurudwaras have received direct governmental support. The concessions to the religious demands offered by the Indian government, and under Mrs. Gandhi's regime, the deliberate encouragement offered to religious leaders of various persuasions only exacerbated the tide of religious nationalism culminating in events and bloodshed that have been very difficult to control. Rather than stemming the tide of a strident BJP, the assassinations of Mrs. Gandhi and Rajiv Gandhi have only provided electoral gains for the BJP and the Sangh Parivar. In the case of India, the problem was not that the actions of a secular state hell bent on purging religious values from public life led to a religious reaction. Quite the contrary, the state was never sufficiently secular and made frequent concessions to religious forces for electoral gains. The dramatic rise of the BJP can hardly be attributed to the presence of a secular and presumably amoral vacuum in the public domain.

The example of modern Egypt provides a good compa-rative scenario (Juergensmeyer, 1995: 385). Following the revolution of 1952, Nasser's support came from both the Muslim Brotherhood and the elite committed to modernism. He was expected to create a Muslim state and a modern secular state at the same time. His tactic was to create an Egypt that was culturally Muslim and politically secular, but the compromise did not succeed. Soon enough the Muslim brotherhood became his foe and labelled him as insufficiently Islamic. Like Nasser, Sadat also raised Muslim expectations by establishing favourable links with the Brotherhood, only to run into loggerheads with them by 1974. The strategy that Sadat adopted was to wear the mantle of Islam, to promote religious schools, and to present himself as the real defender of Islamic values. None of this really worked, and he was always considered a betrayer of Islam by the Brotherhood. His successor, Hosni Mubarak, has been attempting to chart a middle course, making no promises to Muslim activists, but no new secular or socialist departures either (Juergensmeyer, 1995: 385). The parallels with India are quite striking as both Mrs. Gandhi and Rajiv strove very hard to present themselves as defenders of Hindu interests in order to undercut the appeal of the Jan Sangh and then the BJP. But these strategies never really worked, and a strategy of one-upmanship continued by Rao along similar lines in fact contributed to the near disintegration of the Congress Party and the installation of the shaky and insecure coalition government led by the BJP.

THE "RACIALIZATION" OF COMMUNAL IDENTITY AND CONFLICT IN INDIA

The possibility that the current Indian Hindu-Muslim or upper versus lower-caste conflict may be, in a significant sense, a variant of a modern problem of "ethnicity" or "race" is seldom entertain-ed..."racism" is thought of as something the white people do to us. What Indians do to one another are variously described as "communalism", "regionalism" and "casteism" but never "racism". Dipesh Chakrabarty (1994: 145)

The Muslim [is considered] as ever proliferating, sexually prolific, and lusting after Hindu women. Such assumptions have entered deep into middle-class Hindu common sense in many parts of the country, helping to constitute attitudes of approval or compliance about communal violence among many who would never actively participate in riots themselves. Communalism here veers close to everyday racism, with the Muslim – like the black or colored immigrant – felt to be a biological danger, a threat simply by being born, giving birth – even dying. A highly respected gentleman told a group of us investigating the Nizamuddin riot of 1990 that every time a Muslim died, a bit of Mother India's soil was lost through his grave, while the self-effacing Hindu is cremated and does not waste space. Sumit Sarkar (1996)

The Manufacture of Social Identities: Beyond the Obsession with Religion

The dramatic upsurge in conflicts between members of communities whose boundaries are apparently demarcated by religious affiliation is finally beginning to receive the attention of scholars working on India. Despite exceptions such as Beteille (1994), Gupta (1996) Engineer (1989) and Tambiah (1996) sociologists of India were generally spending their intellectual energies on other issues and left it to the historians, economists and political scientists such as Thapar (1989), Brass (1974), Sarkar (1996), Ludden (1996), Basu (1995), Sen (1993; 1996) and Raychaudhuri (2000) to examine the complex structural and material bases of communal conflict. These scholars have recently come under attack by the same sociologists who were earlier preoccupied with other issues but are no longer able to ignore the explosion of conflict and violence in India.

The strident critique of the contextual analyses of communal strife in India has come from a variety of sources, and not all of it is entirely unjustified. However, some sociologists have gone too far in rejecting existing explanations of communalism. For example T.N. Madan (1987:749) has questioned the wisdom of scholars who have focused all their intellectual energies on structural factors in making sense of communal conflict. Madan's critique has been echoed and amplified by others such as Nandy (1985) who claim that existing accounts have reduced religion to an "epi-phenomenon". Such arguments derive largely from an acceptance of a strong version of the secularization thesis. Consequently, scholars such as Madan, Nandy and Veena Das (1989) have focused on the resurgence of fundamentalism on a global scale to argue that in the analysis of communal conflicts, the role of religion ought to be taken seriously. There is no doubt that there is indeed a global resurgence of religious fundamen-talism and scholars such as Arjomand (1984; 1993), Keddie (1998), Juergensmeyer (1993) and Hansen (1999) have analyzed this phenomenon with a great deal of contextual reflexivity. However, the problem with the renewed focus on religion initiated by some scholars working on India is that the intricate dissection of religious texts and doctrines threatens to become the key causal variable for the precipitation of communal conflict. Occasionally, the efflorescence of religious movements has been explained by reference to a social vacuum created by the secularization of institutions and the public sphere in general. In this regard, predictably enough, the omnibus juggernaut of an undifferen-tiated modernity attempting to stamp out the last vestiges of spirituality by forcing amoral secularism onto traditional societies and sensibilities is identified as the source of all the problems (Friedland, 1999). The structural factors that have contributed to such conflicts are systematically underplayed and an internal logic of religion is used to explain communal conflict as a response to the process of secularization. Thus T.N. Madan characterizes secularism as a "gift of Christianity" to argue that while it makes sense in Protestant societies, it simply will not work in presumably religious societies like India. This is apparently so because the "Hindu tradition does not provide us with a dualistic view of the kind which Christianity does" because "the Christian distinction between the sacred and secular domains ...[has] contributed to the success of the modern ideology [of secularism] in the West" (Madan 1994:1095-96). In the same vein Veena Das searches for solutions to communal conflicts by charting out "another notion of morality" based on "reflections on the theory of *purusartha* and *varnadharma*" while urging us to "engage in a critique of the dominant monotheistic traditions of Islam and Christianity" (Das 1989:49-52). If the formulations offered by Madan and Das are to be believed, communal conflict is inextricably linked to the differential social consequences of the ideologies and practices of monotheism, polytheism and secularism. No serious scholar would actually make the claim that differences in theological doctrines are actually precipitating communal conflict, but some seem edging close to a slightly more sophisticated variation on Huntington's "clash of civilizations" theme (Huntington 1996).

In view of the fact that such analyses have already been extensively criticized (Alam 1994; Baber 1996; 1998; Basu, 1995; Beteille, 1994; Brass, 1998; Sarkar, 1996; Sen, 1996; Upadhyaya, 1992; Vanaik 1997, Nanda 2003) the aim of this paper is to move beyond critique in search of alternative accounts. In the dominant discourse, the discursive construction of a "Hindu-Muslim" or "Hindu-Sikh" conflict is firmly entrenched. Such discourses reinforce the idea that differences between specific religious doctrines *per se* generate communal conflicts. The point that some religious doctrines as opposed to others may in theory be more susceptible to successful mobilization by seasoned purveyors of violence is certainly arguable. However, the argument advanced here is that such factors have generally been over-emphasized. Of course, the alternative account offered here is not a definitive one and is open to the usual critiques that constitute part and parcel of the practice of social science.

The argument forwarded here is that at least in the case of India, religious affiliations function as markers for the cons-truction of racialized identities of "imagined communities" (Anderson, 1983). Indeed religious affiliation constitutes the key element for delineating the boundaries between "us" and "them", self and the other. There is enough evidence to indicate that in India religious markers have been deployed historically not just to demarcate ethnic boundaries but also in the long run, to initiate a process of "racialization" of such differences (Miles 1991). The recurring social manufacture and deployment of social identities is a complex process that cannot be grasped by simply focusing on the differences between diverse religious doctrines (Calhoun 1994a; 1994b; 1997; Wallerstein 1991a; 1991b). This is not to claim that religious ideologies are unimportant for making sense of communal conflict in India. In the case of the much-discussed "Hindu-Muslim" issue, certain specific patterns that are strikingly similar to racial conflicts in other social contexts where religion has not been an issue can be identified.

The UN conference on race in Durban, South Africa re-kindled the debate on racism in India. In an opinion piece published in the national daily *The Hindu,* sociologist Andre Beteille strongly rejects the use of the term race because race is not a scientifically valid concept. As he puts it, "we cannot throw out the concept of race by the front door when it is misused for asserting social superiority and bring it in again through the back door to misuse it in the cause of the oppressed. The metaphor of race is a dangerous weapon whether it is used for asserting white supremacy or for making demands on behalf of disadvantaged groups" (Beteille 2001). What seems to have incensed Beteille most was the fact that "not content with condemning racism and racial discrimination, the U.N. now wants to take on `racism, racial discrimination, xenophobia and related intolerance'. It has in its wisdom decided to expand the meeting of racial discrimination to accommodate exclusion or preference `based on race, colour, descent, or national or ethnic origin" (Beteille 2001). As many scholars such as M.S.S. Pandian (2001) and Gail Omvedt (2001) pointed out, categories of race might deploy phenotypical features to create boundaries but they are social constructs of power, ideologies and differential resource allocations. Just because race is not a scientifically valid concept, it does not logically or sociologically follow that racism can be wished out of existence. The fact that there is no Aryan race did not stop the Nazis from coming to power in Germany. To argue that racism cannot exist because there are no scientifically defined categories of race is to miss the point, yet again, of W.I. Thomas' dictum about people's definition of reality having real consequences. Although there is no doubt that racisms of various kinds around the world are not identical in their characteristics and consequences, what they do have in common is the attribution of certain quasi-biological qualities to categories of people that are then used as a basis for stereotyping, discrimination and violence over generations. Needless to add, depending on the restructuring of social and power relations, the boundaries of such racialized collectivities as well as their relative status are always open to contestation and re-negotiation. As a recent empirical study by Varshney (2002) convincingly demonstrates, many of these re-negotiations are contingent upon a number of social, political and economic factors. Using a wealth of empirical data, Varshney's study clearly establishes the futility of focusing on religious differences or presumably primordial ethnic identities alone for providing explanations of communal conflict between Hindus and Muslims. His analysis focuses on the contextual, structural factors to understand the causes of communal conflict in India.

The Self and the Other in Pre-Colonial India

Although the specific conception of the Hindus constituting a "race" and concern over its imminent death became pronounced only during the late nineteenth century, contrary to the dominant view, such concerns pre-date British colonial rule (Bayly 1985; Talbot 1995). As Thapar has argued, conceptions of the "Other" characterised as *mleccha*, have a long and decidedly pre-colonial genealogy in India (Thapar 1971; 1989). More recently, Talbot has criticized the argument that supra-local identities were non-existent prior to the advent of colonial rule (Talbot 1995). While there is no doubt that the development of a wide range of technologies under colonial rule dramatically expanded the possibilities for the construction of specific "imagined commu-nities", there is enough evidence to indicate that the sense of the Hindu "self" and the Muslim "other" was consolidated prior to the onset of colonialism. Pollock's recent study indicates that it was only after the eleventh century with the onset of Muslim invasions that Rama's conflict with the "demonic" Ravana began to take on a new and more widespread ideological role (Pollock 1993). With the continuing incursions by Muslims the narrative of the Ramayana recast the invaders in the role of the demonic Other. The Ramayana, although not absent in the past, was consolidated as the key religious and political narrative and this development was accompanied by a dramatic rise in the emergence of Rama temples and cults. The emergence of clear-cut Hindu versus Muslim identity can be located in this period and continued with the consolidation of a Muslim rule in other parts of India. The most dramatic instance of demonization of Muslims is evident in the immediate aftermath of the collapse of the *Kakatiya* dynasty in the Andhra region as a consequence of the expansion of the *Delhi Sultanate*. The earliest instance of negative representations of Muslims in Andhra records appear in the first quarter of the fourteenth century, and continue apace as by 1325, virtually all of southern India was under Muslim rule. A copper inscription, written and issued between 1325 and 1350, recounts the death of the king Prataparudra and the rise of the forces of evil. The inscription goes on to paint a picture of the persecution and slaying of Brahmins, the destruction of temples, confiscation of tax-exempt Brahmin villages, and the proliferation of wine and beef consumption (Talbot 1995:696-7).

Some historians seeking to provide a Hindu perspective have accepted the account in the inscription as literal truth. However, as Talbot has pointed out, the depiction of Muslims and the consequences of their actions conform too closely to a popular literary convention to be accepted uncritically as actual fact (Talbot

1995:697). The inscription in question deploys the narrative of the *puranas* composed in the first millennium. It predicts the coming to an end of *Kali's* age leading to the usurpation of political power by foreigners, a lack of respect for the *Vedas*, for Brahmins and the hierarchical order of the caste system. The *puranas* capture the anxiety of their Brahmin composers particularly at a time when Buddhism was in a process of consolidation. The incursion of Muslim rulers precipitated such anxieties about the restructuring of the established hierarchical order of power and privilege, provoking a dramatic deployment of specific social memories to deal with the future. The earlier discourse of the *mlechha* or the barbarian usually referred to all social groups bereft of Brahmanical norms. The term *Yavanas* deriving from Ionian or the "Greeks" who controlled large tracts of north-western India in the second century BC, was also used to describe "the barbarians" (Thapar 1989:224). The same terms were revived in early medieval India in an attempt to insert the Muslims in a pre-existing discursive formation. Like the *Yavanas* of the past, Muslims were cast in the role of agents bent on disrupting the existing hierarchical structures that ensured Brahminical privilege and power. The Muslims, as constructed by the Brahman scribes, were repositioned as the demons of the ancient narratives, locked in a Manichean battle against the forces of good (Talbot 1995: 699). The emergent difference, constituted by the narratives of the *puranas,* between the Hindu Self and the Muslim Other was obviously not primarily religious in nature, but represented reactions to declining status and material privileges of the dominant strata. That the Muslim Other was never represented as Islamic or Muslim, but invariably as Turk, Persian and Greek is revealing. Inscriptions from other parts of the country of this period also do not refer to Islamic religion or the Islamic affiliation of the Turks, and the sense of difference clearly did not emanate from purely religious factors (Talbot 1995:701). This point is significant in the context of the tendency of some scholars to focus on the content of religious doctrines in discussions of communalism.

The consolidation of a sense of the Hindu Self and Muslim Other was also spurred by the emergence of a number of local rulers in Andhra who, after the incursions of the Delhi *sultanate*, carved out regions of governance for themselves. Some of these new rulers attempted to force a connection with the earlier *Kakatiya* dynasty, and granted lands and villages to Brahmins in order to legitmize their rule. Each such land grant further demonized the Muslims. The immediate goal was to produce narratives of perceived injustices of the past (Talbot 1995:703). In these narratives, there is no hint of the religious factor as the main motivation behind the constructions of the Self and Other. It was precisely in this period of instability and uncertainty that the legitimation of the power of the Andhra kings was sought through the modification and mobilization of pre-existing discourses of the Other to demonize Muslims as a separate category. Indeed, from the early fifteenth to the mid sixteenth century, a period of relative stability, not only was there no anti-Muslim rhetoric, but the inscriptional sources actually indicate narratives of praise for Muslim warriors and the political establishment (Talbot 1995: 706). In the constitution of the Other, material consideration of declining power and privilege rather than religious distinctions and doctrinal differences played a greater role.

The Idea of a Hindu "Race" and Alarm over its Impending Death

In addition to the conflicts in the medieval period, British colonialism provided a major impetus for the dramatic consolidation of Hindu and Muslim identities (Trautmann, 1997; Ballantine,

2002). Orientalist scholarship, focusing among other things on the concept of an Indo-Aryan linguistic family, the Aryan Race and the Golden Age of Hinduism presumably terminated by the Muslim invasions contributed to the "raciali-zation", in the sense discussed by Miles (1991), Ratcliffe (1994), Ignatiev (1995), Wacquant (1997) and Wieviorka (1995) of communal identity. Spurred by the structural and ideological impact of colonial rule, a number of Hindu activists drew on the writings of Orientalist scholars on India to call for the resurrection of the "Golden age" that was according to colonialist narratives, destroyed by the alien "race" of Muslim invaders. The "raciali-zation" of identities through the construction and deployment of an identifiable discourse of quasi-biological, immutable differences was well underway. As early as the 1860's Swami Dayanand Saraswati, founder of the Hindu revivalist organization, the *Arya Samaj*, drew on Max Muller's translation of the *Vedas* to articulate the idea that the Hindus were clearly the descendants of the *Aryas* who themselves were an elect and primordial people. Dayanand concluded that the *Aryas* originating from Tibet, settled in *Aryavarta* or north India before dominating the world (Jaffrelot 1997:330). Sarda (1906) sought to trace the Hindu "colonization of the world" and to demonstrate that in the past, much of the world was dominated and eventually peopled by members of the "Hindu race". These narratives were further amplified by many other Hindu ideologues of the period. There was of course considerable variation and some narratives were more nuanced than others. However, a limited number of dominant themes generated the poly-vocality on the surface. U.N. Mukherji represented a particularly influential voice of the period. His text *Hindus – a Dying Race* (1909) sought to ring the alarm bells about the imminent demise of a once dominant Hindu "race". Elaborating on the specific qualities of Muslims, Mukherji held them up as a community worthy of emulation because the "superiority of the Mohammedans is entirely due to their religious revival and systematic moral training." (Mukherji 1909, cited in Datta 1993:1307). This rhetorical strategy of what Jaffrelot (1996) refers to as the simultaneous emulation and stigmatisation of Muslims continues to be a staple element of contemporary *Hindutva* discourse. Mukherji traced the decline of the "Hindu race" and the proliferation of Muslims to the presumed proclivity of Hindu widows for marrying Muslim males. (Datta 1993:1307). Skilfully deploying existing stereotypical images of the Muslim male as particularly lustful and sexually driven, a construction that can be traced to Renaissance Europe (Said 1978), Mukherji sought to simultaneously create and tap into a reservoir of guilt among the presumably effete Hindu male who was accused of being unable to defend his motherland and "his women". This view of the Hindu male was parasitical on the dominant British stereotypical view of the Hindu Bengali male. Macaulay had already declared that "the physical organisation of the Bengalee is feeble even to effeminacy....his pursuits are sedentary, his limbs delicate, his movement languid." (Macaulay cited in Gordon 1974: 6). The colonial construction of the presumed effeminacy of Hindu males, their physical weakness and "emasculation" was to become a dominant feature of the Hindu nationalist discourse. In 1899, Swami Vivekananda while discussing the "problems" of Hindus had focused on the "physical weakness which was responsible for one-third of their problems." Much later, Nathuram Godse, the assassin of Gandhi had rejected the latter's emphasis on non-violence because it "would ultimately result in the emasculation of the Hindu community." This fear of emasculation represents the inversion of precisely those qualities that the Muslim males were presumably endowed with. Not surprisingly the first reaction of

Bal Thackeray, the leader of the aggressively militant organization *Shiv Sena* to the Indian nuclear tests of May 1998, was a gleeful "we have proven that we are not emasculated." Nor is it surprising that a large proportion of the energies of the RSS, another militant Hindu organization are devoted to the male body and the cultivation of hyper-masculinity (Alter, 1992; Sinha 1995; Basu, 1994). The recent release of prisoners by the Indian government in exchange for hostages of the hijacking incident in Afghanistan prompted the predictable response by Rajendra Singh - the leader of the RSS - that Hindus have yet again proven to be "cowards".

Mukherji's panic at the presumed decline of the Hindu race and the alarming fecundity of Muslims, was not without its antecedents nor has this idea disappeared in contemporary India. The antecedents of this argument can be found in colonialist accounts as well as in the writings of one of the most revered figures for the supporters of the discourse of *Hindutva*. Writing in 1899, Swami Vivekananda who is currently being pressed into service by the ideologues of *Hindutva* argued "when the Mohammadens first came to India, what a great number of Hindus were there, but mark, how today they have dwindled down! Everyday they will become less and less till they totally disappear." (Vivekananda 1962:373). This dominant view of the Muslim proclivity for producing children as a calculated demographic strategy for outnumbering the Hindus is an argument that continues to resurface in contemporary *Hindutva* discourse. Indeed this conception of reproduction as a strategy for eventual domination has been ascribed to most minorities through history and across cultures (Patterson, 1998). Similar writings, aimed at demonstrating the superiority of the Hindu race and their domination of the world, proliferated during this period. Aimed at shoring up self-esteem at a time of colonial domination, these thinkers ironically re-deployed the same discourse propagated by the British administrators to justify colonial subjugation. This discourse originating from the work of the early Orientalists like William Jones and Prinsep focused on the presumed common linguistic and racial origins of the European and Indian population. As mentioned earlier, a key motif of this discourse was the idea of a Golden Age of Hinduism whose sudden decline was causally connected to the Muslim invasions. From the British administrators' point of view, such a discourse of a once mighty Hindu nation and race in decline provided ample ideological justification for colonial rule as the prime and perhaps only agency for its eventual regeneration (Baber 1996).

In the context of a loss of status during colonial rule, elements of colonialist ideas such as the concept of the Aryan race were selectively retrieved, narrativized and deployed to articulate the ides of a "Hindu race". Imparting a concrete form to views that were widespread at the time and continue to inform contemporary *Hindutva* discourse, Swami Vivekananda wrote in 1899:

> Now the Mohammedans are the crudest in this respect and the most sectarian. Their watchword is: "There is one God and Mohammed is his Prophet". Everything beyond that not only is bad, but must be destroyed forthwith; at a moment's notice, every man or woman who does not exactly believe in that must be killed; everything that does not belong to this worship must be immediately broken; every book that teaches anything else must be burnt. From the Pacific to the Atlantic, for five hundred years blood ran all over the world. That is Mohammedanism. (Viveknanda 1972 Vol. 4:126).

In line with his goal of propagating a universal religion of Advaita that would incorporate elements of all other religions, he did qualify the above remarks by adding "nevertheless, among these Mohammedans, wherever there was a philosophic man, he was sure to protest these cruelties" (Vivekananda 1972 Vol. 4: 126). A few pages later, the effect of the qualification was effectively nullified by the following graphic observation:

> To the Mussulman, the Jews or the Christians are not objects of extreme detestation; they are, at the worst, men of little faith. But not so the Hindu. According to him, the Hindu is idolatrous, the hateful Kafir; hence in this life he deserves to be butchered; and in the next, eternal hell is in store for him. The utmost the Mussulman kings could do as a favour to the priestly class – the spiritual guides of these Kafirs – was to allow them somehow to pass their life silently and wait for the last moment. This was again sometimes considered too much kindness! If the religious ardour of any king was a little more uncommon, there would immediately follow arrangements for a great Yajna of Kafir-slaughter!" (Vivekananda 1972 Vol. 4:446).

After ostensibly expressing admiration for the concept of "universal brotherhood" in "Mohammedanism" by stating that "Mohammad by his life showed that among Mohammedans there should be perfect equality and brotherhood", Vivekananda went on to question its application in practice in the following terms:

> Mohammedans talk of universal brotherhood but what comes out of that in reality? Why anybody who is not a Mohammedan will not be admitted into the brotherhood; he will more likely have his throat cut" (Vivekananda 1972: Vol. 4: 133; Vol. 2:380).

In a letter addressed to Mohammad Sarfaraz Husain, Vivekananda deploys the dominant stereotype of Muslims presumably congenitally endowed with physical might but lacking in intellect, to argue that "for our motherland a junction of the two great systems, Hinduism and Islam – Vedanta brain and Islam body – is the only hope. I see in my mind's eye the future perfect India rising out of this chaos and strife, glorious and invincible, with a Vedanta brain and Islam body" (Vivekananda 1993:380). In the same letter, he goes on to proclaim the universality of Advaitism since it is "the last word of religion and thought and the only position from which one can look upon all religions and sects with love." Regardless of the context in which Vivekananda enunciated these views, they were pursued by the inheritors of this tradition. Such formulations also constitute the staple of newsgroups on the internet and other media (Rai, 1995; Guneratne, 1998).

These formulations were further amplified in a one-dimensional manner by the future ideologues of Hindutva. V.D. Savarkar, who had spent some time in England, drew upon the writings of Herbert Spencer, Huxley and the zoologist Ernest Haeckel, to compose the agenda setting text *Hindutva – Who is a Hindu?* in 1923. Referring to the Hindus, Savarkar claimed that:

> They are not only a race-jati…all Hindus claim to have in their veins the blood of the mighty race incorporated with and descended from the vedic fathers…(Savarkar 1969:100).

Discussing the various castes and communities that constituted Hinduism, Savarkar insisted that "we are all Hindus and own a common blood. We feel that the same ancient blood that coursed through the veins of Ram and Krishna, Buddha and Maha-vir…. courses throughout Hindudom from vein to vein, pulsates from heart to heart" (Savarkar 1969:89). While in London, Savarkar had introduced the ritual of a daily pledge to be recited by the inmates of India House. This ritual obsessed with obliterating pluralism as the precondition for nationalism, consisted of collectively chanting "One God, one nation, one language, one race, one form, one hope." The view that pluralism in any form is inimical to the construction of a "strong" nation, derived from Western theories on the issue, is evident in the pronouncements of many contemporary ideologues of *Hindutva*. In 1938, during the course of a public speech in Delhi, V.D. Savarkar, congratulated Hitler for pursuing his policies. The official newspaper of the same organization, the *Hindu Outlook* continued to shower praise on Franco, Mussolini and Hitler throughout this period (Jaffrelot 1996:336). Indeed, the next president of the *Hindu Mahasabha*, K.P. Moonje, had in fact met Hitler and Mussolini during this period and on his return to India, established a military school in Nasik that was organized along the lines of fascist schools of Italy (Jaffrelot 1995: 336).

The formation of the quasi-fascist organization RSS in 1925, complete with a uniform, compulsory drills for members and a signature salute for "the leader" consolidated the constitution of boundaries of the Hindu "race". The issue of a Hindu race figured prominently in the influential tract *We or Our Nationhood Defined* (1938) penned by the leader of the RSS, Guru Golwalkar. This is the defining text for many contemporary militant *Hindutva* organizations and continues to exercise strong influence on the institutional mind of the BJP. Expressing admiration for Hitler and his policy of racial genocide, Golwalkar wrote:

> German pride has now become the topic of the day. To keep up the purity of the Race and its culture, Germany has shocked the world by purging the country of the semitic Races – the Jews. Race pride at its highest has been manifested here. Germany has also shown how well nigh impossible it is for races and cultures, having differences going to the root, to be assimilated into one united whole, a good lesson for us in Hindusthan to learn and profit by. (Golwalkar 1947:43).

Golwalkar held up the Nazi model of a nation infused with special racial qualities as a strategy for regenerating the Hindu nation that according to him had once been powerful, but was now in ruins. Referring to the German experience he wrote:

> The ancient Race spirit which prompted the Germanic tribes to over-run the whole of Europe, has re-risen in modern Germany. With the result that the nation perforce follows aspirations, predetermined by the traditions left by its depredatory ancestors. Even so with us: our Race spirit has once again roused itself as is evidenced by the race of spiritual giants we have produced, and who today stalk the world in serene majesty (Golwalkar 1947:21).

As Jaffrelot (1996) has argued, in his formulations Golwalkar drew explicitly on the eugenic core of European fascism. Golwalkar's demand that minorities, defined here in racial terms, must either assimilate or be eliminated, was derived from a fairly long tradition of racism in Europe and its echoes in contemporary India can be found in the slogan – *Babar ki santaan, jao pakistan ya kabristan* (Progeny of Babar, chose Pakistan or the graveyard).

In the above ideological reconstruction, the emphasis on a specific conception of the Hindu "race" is fused with a particular notion of the nation to explain the causes of decline from a presumed Vedic Golden Age. The goal is the regeneration of both race and nation. In re-defining India as a Hindu nation, Golwalkar explicitly drew upon the racial theories of Gumplovicz and Bluntschli's *The Theory of the State* to argue:

> A nation is a union of masses of men of different conceptions and social states, in hereditary society of common spirit, feeling and race bound together especially by a language and customs in a common civilization which gives them a sense of unity and distinction from all foreigners, quite apart from the bond of the state (Golwalkar 1947:21).

The ideas of Savarkar and Golwalkar, although formulated over sixty years ago, continue to inform the discourse of the amalgamation of parties and organizations popularly known as the *Sangh Parivar*.

"Racisms", Nationalisms and Communities

It could be argued that communal conflict is yet another example of ethnic rather than racial strife and this is indeed true to a certain degree (Varshney 2002). The recent debates about whether the contested concepts of "race" and "racism" continue to be meaningful or ought to be abandoned in favour of the concept of "ethnicity" highlights the complexities of this issue (Smith, 2002; Modood, Berthoud, Nazroo, 2002) Thus the delineation of "race" is expected to involve the conferment of social significance to distinctive phenotypical traits. In the case of Hindus and Muslims however, there are no such phenotypical attributes that visibly demarcate one community from the other. However, distinctive phenotypical markers have never been essential for the task of "racialising" communities and ascribing fixed, immutable attributes to them. Formulating the issue from very different and sometimes even contradictory perspectives, scholars have emphasized the processes under which collectivities are produced and racialized. While refusing to let go of phenotypical characteristics, Rex argues that racism can be found in any situation where:

> The inequalities and differentiation inherent in a social structure are related to physical and cultural criteria of an ascriptive kind and are rationalized in terms of deterministic belief systems, of which the most usual in recent years has made reference to biological science (Rex 1970:39).

This focus on a "deterministic belief system" when combined with specific structural contexts provides a powerful conceptual framework for making sense of the multiplicity of ways in which social identities can be "racialized" in specific social and political formations. Incorporating a class dimension, Miles seeks to focus on "racialization" as a dynamic process at work in all "those instances where social relations between people have been structured by the signification of human biological characteristics in such a way as to define and construct differentiated social collectivities" (Miles 1989: 75). Moving away from phenotypical attributes, Balibar has introduced the notion of "cultural racism" whose "dominant theme is not biological heredity but the insurmountability of cultural differences, a racism which, at first sight, does not postulate the superiority of certain groups or peoples in relation to others but "only" the harmfulness of abolishing frontiers, the incompatibility of life-styles and traditions." (Balibar 1991:21).

This conceptual distance from phenotypical characteristics as essential ingredients of race opens up possibilities for analyzing the diversity of ways in which racism works overtly and covertly even though race as such does not exist (Anthias, 1992; 1998; Patterson, 1998). These developments point to the importance of specific historical and political conditions under which racial divisions are consolidated in specific combination with other collectivities such as nations and classes. As Goldberg puts it, these reformulations have contributed to a situation where "the presumption of a single monolithic racism is being displaced by a mapping of the multifarious historical formulations of racisms" (Goldberg 1988). To understand this process, one need only examine the various ways in which constructions such as the "white" or "black" race have been constituted and re-constituted through history, depending on shifting configurations of power relations and availability of ideological resources at hand (Roediger, 1992; 1994; Gates 1997). Despite its close association with phenotypical difference as the primary marker, most social scientists would agree that race is a social construct that is sustained, reproduced and transformed through its intersection with existing institutional arrangements, ideologies and discursive formations (Li, 1999). As such, the work of essentializing entire groups of people with immutable, inheritable and quasi-biological behavioural attributes contributes to the process of constituting and simultaneously "racializing" what might indeed be nothing more than cultural differences (Miles 1991; Appiah 1990; Goldberg 1990; Balibar 1990; Omi and Winant, 1994; Bonilla-Silva 1997; Marx, 1998; Wacquant 1997; Solomos and Back, 1994; Brah, 1994, Jasper, 1997). The most dramatic example of this process is of course the construction of Jewish and Aryan race in Nazi Germany. The ideologically constructed phenotypical markers for each "race" were frequently reversed. As has been frequently noted, Hitler himself failed to conform to the phenotypical expectations of the "Aryan race", but the absence of these phenotypical markers did not prevent the social construction of such markers and their deployment for the categorization of the German population into distinct races. Singapore also constitutes a good example of this logic – or lack thereof – of this process where the population is divided into four "races", the Chinese, the Malays, the Indians and the "Others"! In both popular and official discourse, these "races" are imbued with quasi-biological essences (Benjamin 1975). Usually such essentializing of differences has quasi-biological overtones, even though this is not a precondition for the construction of racial difference and its conceptions of superiority and inferiority. In the case of India however, biological overtones in the construction of race are not entirely absent. Savarkar's views on the most recent Muslim converts in India is particularly revealing. As he puts it, "he possesses – in certain cases they do – pure Hindu blood; especially if he is the first convert to Mohammedanism he must be allowed to claim to inherit the blood of Hindu parents" (Savarkar 1969:101).

Racism of Domination versus Racism of Extermination?

In a recent contribution Jaffrelot, whose work represents the most coherent analysis of communalism, labels the ideology of *Hindutva* a "racism of domination [rather] than a racism of extermination" (Jaffrelot 1996:30). Jaffrelot's argument is that in *Hindutva* discourses, the Other is not excluded, but integrated to the national body-politic at a subordinate rank. In this respect, Jaffrelot concurs with Pandey's view that such strategies of exclusion or inclusion through subordination represent a form of "upper caste racism" (Pandey 1993: 252). While it is true that a racism of extermination is not the dominant strain within the *Hindutva* discourses, Golwalkar's enthusiastic approval of Hitler's policies indicates that this element is not entirely absent. Indeed the logic of racism of extermination has manifested itself during "riots" involving the two communities and the state apparatuses. It is easier to agree with Chakrabarty who has expressed strong disagreement with the dominant view that whatever Indians do to one another can be described variously as "communalism", "regionalism", "casteism" etc. but never racism. This is usually because conveniently enough, "racism is thought of something the white people do to us" (Chakrabarty1994:145). As Solomon and Back (1994: 151) point out, "contemporary manifestations of race are coded in a language which aims to circumvent accusations of racism. In the new racism race is coded as culture…the semantics of race are produced by a complex set of inter-discursive processes where the language of culture and nation invokes hidden racial narratives." Provided one accepts the idea that racial differences are not directly derived from phenotypical characteristics but are indeed socially constructed, one can see that the logic at work in India is similar to the logic of racial conflict, with its attendant conflicts over resources, residential segregation, violently enforced endogamy, armory of stereotypes, myth-making and invented histories. In the Indian case of course, the racialization of boundaries has been articulated with a very explosive mix. The *Hindutva* strain of exclusive nationalism deliberately seeks to either exclude or include the Muslims as a subordinate category. It is also a non-territorial nationalism that seeks to mobilize Hindus who in the world of Lala Lajpat Rai are "a nation in themselves, because they represent a type of civilization all their own" (Jaffrelot 1996: 19). This strain of exclusive nationalism is in marked contrast to the other inclusive, modernist, Nehruvian secular nationalism that is under attack, not just by the *Hindutva* ideologues, but also by a group of highly visible and prolific scholars pre-occupied with grandiose projects of interrogating an undifferentiated modernity and its discontents (Nandy 1985; Madan 1987; Das, 1989).

In conclusion, what appears to be a conflict rooted in the clash of cultures, religions and civilizations, can be better understood as a specific form of "cultural racism" at work. "Cultural racism" involving the creation and sustenance of boundaries, stereotypes, residential segregation and endogamy is of course not restricted to the two major religious groups, Hindus and Muslims in India. It is very much in evidence within these imagined religious communities, exhibiting similar characteris-tics and leading to frequent riots and violence that serve to recreate and reinforce such boundaries. Within the imagined Hindu community exist divisions, most noticeably between the Dalits and the upper-castes but these "racialized" divisions are not restricted to these groups alone (Cox 1959; Kothari, 1994). Among the Muslims in India, similar divisions can be found between the Shias and Sunnis, as well as other status distinctions within these two major categories. Finally, the racialization of religious distinctions is certainly not restricted to India. The conflict between Catholics and Protestants in Northern Ireland as well as the culmination of the idea of an Aryan and Jewish "race" in Nazi Germany are to a large extent, variation on the theme developed in this paper – "racism without race". The current obsession with the presumed shortcomings of the stated state policy of secularism (Nandy, 1985; Madan, 1987; Beteille 1994; Baber, 1996) hinders the analysis of communalism in contemporary India. In addition to studies that have focused on the mix of political and sociological factors that have contributed to communal conflicts, a re-conceptualisation of communal groups as "racialised' categories could help in at least identifying the right questions that ought to be posed.

BIBLIOGRAPHY

Ahmad, Aijaz. 1992. *In Theory: Classes, Nations, Literatures.* New York: Verso.

——. 1993a. "Fascism and National Culture: Reading Gramsci in the Days of Hindutva", *Social Scientist*, 238-39, March/April.

——. 1993b. "Culture, Community, Nation: On the Ruins of Ayodhya", *Social Scientist*, 242-43, July/August.

Ahmad, Imtiaz. 1976. "For a Sociology of India" in T.N. Madan (ed.) *Muslim Communities of South Asia.* New Delhi: Vikas.

Alam, J. 1994. "Tradition in India Under Interpretive Stress: Interrogating its Claims", *Thesis Eleven*, 39:19-38.

Alter, Joseph. 1992. *The Wrestler's Body: Identity and Ideology in North India.* Berkeley: University of California Press.

Anderson, B. 1983. *Imagined Communities: Reflections on the Origin and Spread of Nationalism.* London: Verso.

Anthias, F. 1992. "Connecting Race and Ethnic Phenomena", *Sociology*, 26,3:421-38.

——. 1998. "Rethinking Social Divisions: Some Notes Towards a Theoretical Framework", *Sociological Review*, 46,3:505-535.

Appiah, A.K. 1990. "Racisms" in David Theo Goldberg (ed.) *Anatomy of Racism.* Minneapolis: University of Minnesota Press.

Arjomand, S.A. (ed.) 1984. *From Nationalism to Revolutionary Islam.*

London: Macmillan.

—— (ed.). 1993. *The Political Dimensions of Religion.* Albany: State University of New York.

Baber, Z. 1996a. *The Science of Empire: Scientific Knowledge, Civilization and Colonial Rule in India.* Albany: State University of New York Press.

——. 1996b. "After Ayodhya: Politics, Religion and the Emerging Culture of Academic Anti-Secularism", *Dialectical Anthropology*, 21,3:317-343.

——. 1998. "Communal Conflict and the Nostalgic Imagination in India", *Journal of Contemporary Asia*, 28,1:27-44.

——. 2000. "Religious Nationalism, Violence and the *Hindutva* Movement in India", *Dialectical Anthropology*, 25,1:61-76.

Bailey, F.G. 1959. "For a Sociology of India?" *Contributions to Indian Sociology* 3:88-101.

——. 1992. "Religion and Religiosity: Ideas and their Use", *Contri-butions to Indian Sociology* 25,2:211-32.

Balibar, E. 1990. "Paradoxes of Universality", in David T. Goldberg (ed.) *Anatomy of Racism.* Minneapolis: University of Minnesota Press.

——. 1991. "Is there a neo-racism?" in Etienne Balibar and Immanuel Wallerstein I. (ed.), *Race, Nation, Class: Ambiguous Identities.* New York: Verso.

Ballantyne, T. 2002. *Orientalism and Race: Aryanism in the British Empire.* New York: Palgrave.

Barker, Eileen, James A. Beckford and Karel Dobbelaere (eds). 1993. *Secularisation, Rationalism and Sectarianism: Essays in Honour of Bryan Wilson.* Oxford: Oxford University Press.

Barnett, M.R. 1976. *The Politics of Cultural Nationalism in South India.* Princeton: Princeton University Press.

Basu, A. 1994. "Feminism Inverted: The Real Women and Gendered Imagery of Hindu Nationalism", *Bulletin of Concerned Asian Scholars* 25,4.

——. 1995. "Why Local Riots are not Simply Local", *Theory and Society*, 24:35-78.

Basu, Amrita. 1997. "Reflections on Community Conflicts and the State in India", *Journal of Asian Studies* 56,2:391-97.

Basu, Amrita and Atul Kohli. 1997. "Community Conflicts and the State in India", *Journal of Asian Studies* 56,2:320-324.

Basu, Kaushik and Sanjay Subramaniam (eds.). 1996. *Unravelling the Nation: Sectarian Conflict and India's Secular Identity.* New Delhi: Penguin.

Bauman, Zygmunt. 1987. "The Importance of Being Marxist", in William Outhwaite and Michael Mulkay (eds.), *Social Theory and Social Criticism: Essays in Honour of Tom Bottomore.* Oxford: Blackwell.

Bayly, C.A. 1985. "The Pre-History of Communalism? Religious Conflict in India, 1700-1860", *Modern Asian Studies*, 19,2.

Bellah, Robert and Phillip Hammond. 1980. *Varieties of Civil Religion.* New York: Harper and Row.

Bellah, Robert. 1970. *Beyond Belief: Essays on Religion in a Post-Traditional World.* New York: Harper and Row.

Benjamin, G. 1975. "The Cultural Logic of Singapore's Multiracialism", Singapore: Department of Sociology Working Papers, National University of Singapore.

Beteille, A. 1994. "Secularism and Intellectuals", *Economic and Political Weekly*, March 5:559-566.

——. 2001. "Race and Caste", *The Hindu*, 10 March 2001.

——. 1994. "Secularism and Intellectuals", *Economic and Political Weekly* March 5, 559-566.

——. 1974. "Sociology and Ethnosociology", *International Social Science Journal*, 26,4:703-4.

——. 1986. "Individualism and Equality", *Current Anthroplogy*, 27,2:121-28.

——. 1991. "The Reproduction of Inequality", *Contributions to Indian Sociology*, 25,1:30-46,

——. 1991. *Society and Politics in India: Essays in a Comparative Perspective.* London: Athlone Press.

——. 1994. "Secularism and Intellectuals", *Economic and Political Weekly*, March 5: 559-566

Bilgrami, Akeel. 1993. "What is a Muslim? Fundamental Commitment and Cultural Identity" in Gyanendra Pandey (ed.) *Hindus and Others: The Question of Identity in India Today.* New Delhi: Viking.

——. 1994. "Two Concepts of Secularism", *Yale Journal of Criticism*, 7.

Bonilla-Silva, E. 1997. "Rethinking Racism", *American Sociological Review*, 62,3:456-479.

Brah, A. 1994. "Time, Place, and Others: Discourses of Race, Nation, and Ethnicity", *Sociology*, 28,3:805-813.

Brass, P. 1974. *Language, Religion and Politics in North India.* Cambridge: Cambridge University Press.

——. 1998. "Secularism out of its place", *Contributions to Indian Sociology*, 32,2:485-505.

Calhoun, C. 1994. "Social Theory and the Politics of Identity", in Craig Calhoun (ed.) *Social Theory and the Politics of Identity.* Cambridge: Blackwell.

——. 1997. *Nationalism.* Buckingham: Open University Press.

—— (ed.). 1994. *Social Theory and the Politics of Identity.* Cambridge: Blackwell.

Chakrabarty, D. 1994. "Modernity and Ethnicity in India", *South Asia*, 17.

Chatterjee, Partha. 1986. *Nationalist Thought and the Colonial World: A Derivative Discourse?* London: Zed Press.

Cox, Oliver. 1959. *Caste, Class and Race.* New York: Monthly Review Press.

Das V. 1989. "Differences and Division as Designs for Life", in Carla Borden (ed.) *Contemporary Indian Tradition: Voices on Cultures, Nature and the Challenge of Change.* Washington: Smithsonian Institution Press.

Das, V. and Nandy, A. 1986. "Violence, Victimhood and the Language of Silence" in Veena Das (ed.) *The Word and the World.* Delhi: Sage.

Datta, P.K. 1993. "Dying Hindus: Production of Hindu Communal Commonsense in Early 20th Century Bengal", *Economic and Political Weekly,* June 19:1305-19.

Dumont, Louis and Pocock, D. 1957. "For a Sociology of India", *Contributions to Indian Sociology* 1,1:7-22.

Embree, Ainslie. 1990. *Utopias in Conflict.* Berkeley: University of California Press.

Engineer, Asghar Ali. 1989. *Communalism and Communal Violence in India.* Delhi: Ajanta.

—— (ed.). 1992. *Politics of Confrontation.* Delhi: Ajanta.

—— (ed.). 1984. *Communal Riots in Post-Independence India.* Hyderabad: Sangam Books.

Friedland, R. 1999. "When God Walks in History: The Institutional Politics of Religious Nationalism", *International Sociology* 14,3:301-319.

Gates, E.N. (ed.) 1997. *Racial Classification and History.* New York: Garland.

Giddens, Anthony. 1985. *The Nation State and Violence.* Berkeley: University of California Press.

Godse, N. (ed.) 1977. *May it Please Your Honour: Statement of Nathuram Godse, 8 November 1948,* Pune.

Goldberg, D.T. 1990. "The Social Formation of Racist Discourse", in David Theo Goldberg (ed.) *Anatomy of Racism.* Minneapolis: University of Minnesota Press.

—— (ed.). 1990. *Anatomy of Racism,* Minneapolis: University of Minnesota Press.

Golwalkar, M.S. [1938]1947. *We, or Our Nationhood Defined.* Nagpur.

Gordon, L. 1974. *Bengal: The Nationalist Movement.* Delhi: Manohar.

Guneratne, A. R. 1998. "Mediating the Rise of Neo-Nationalism in India: Television, Cinema and Carnival", *Social Identities,* 4/2: 263-81.

Gupta, D. 1996. *The Context of Ethnicity: Sikh Identity in a Comparative*

Perspective, New York: Oxford University Press.

Gupta, Dipankar. "The Indispensable Centre: Ethnicity and Politics in the Nation-State", *Journal of Contemporary Asia* Vol. 26 (1990):521-39.

Gupta, Dipankar, Sumanta Banerjee, Dinesh Mohan, Gautam Navlakha. 1988. "Punjab: Communalised Beyond Politics", *Economic and Political Weekly,* August 13, 1988:1677-1684.

Hansen, T. B. 1999. *The Saffron Wave: Democracy and Hindu Nationalism in Modern India.* Princeton: Princeton University Press.

Hanson, Thomas Blom. 1996. "Recuperating Masculinity: Hindu Nationalism, Violence and the Exorcism of the Muslim Other", *Critique of Anthropology* 16(2):137-172.

Hay, Stephen. (ed.) 1988. *Sources of Indian Tradition,* Volume II. New York: Columbia University Press.

Huntington, S. 1996. *The Clash of Civlizations and the Remaking of World Order.* New York: Simon and Schuster.

Ignatiev, N. 1995. *How the Irish Became White.* New York: Routledge.

Irschick, Eugene. *Politics and Social Conflict in South India: the Non-Brahman Movement and Tamil Separatism.* Berkeley: University of California Press, 1969.

Jaffrelot, C. 1995. "The Idea of Hindu Race" in Peter Robb (ed.) *The Concept of Race in South Asia.* Delhi: Oxford University Press.

Jaffrelot, C. 1996. *The Hindu Nationalist Movement in India.* New York: Columbia University Press.

Jaffrelot, Christophe. 1996. *The Hindu Nationalist Movement in India.* New York: Columbia University Press.

Jasper, J.M. 1997. *The Art of Moral Protest.* Chicago: University of Chicago Press.

Jeffery, Roger and Patricia Jeffery. 1994. "The Bijnor Riots, October 1990: Collapse of a Mythical Special Relationship?" *Economic and Political Weekly,* March 5, 1994:551-558.

Juergensmeyer, M. 1993. *The New Cold War? Religious Nationalism Confronts the Secular State,* Berkeley: University of California Press.

Juergensmeyer, Mark. "The New Religious State", *Comparative Politics* 1995:379-391.

Keddie, N. 1998. "The New Religious Politics: Where, When, and Why do 'Fundamentalisms' Appear", *Comparative Studies in Society and History*, 40,4:696-723.

Kiernan, Victor G. *History, Classes and Nation-States.* Cambridge: Polity Press, 1988.

Kohli, Atul. "Can Democracies Accommodate Ethnic Nationalism: The Rise and Decline of Self-Determination Movement", *Journal of Asian Studies* 1997, 56,2:325-344.

Kurien, Prema. 1994. "Colonialism and Ethnogenesis", *Theory and Society* 23(3):385-418.

Lardinois, Roland. 1996. "The Genesis of Louis Dumont's Anthropology: The 1930's in France Revisited", *Comparative Studies in South Asia, Africa and the Middle East* XVI, 1:27-40.

Larson, Gerald. *India's Agony Over Religion.* Albany: State University of New York Press, 1995.

Lechner, Frank. 1991. "The Case Against Secularization: A Rebuttal", *Social Forces* 69(4):1103-1119.

Li, P. (ed.) 1999. *Race and Ethnic Relations in Canada.* Toronto: Oxford University Press.

Ludden, D. (ed.) 1996. *Contesting the Nation: Religion, Community, and the Politics of Democracy in India.* Philadelphia: University of Pennsylvania Press.

Madan, T. N. "Secularism in its Place", *Journal of Asian Studies* 46,4 (1987):747-59.

Madan, T.N. 1994. "Secularism and the Intellectuals", *Economic and Political Weekly,* April 30, pp. 1095-96.

Mann, E. A. 1992. Boundaries and Identities: Muslims, Work and Status in Aligarh. New Delhi: Sage.

Marriott, McKim. (ed.) 1990. *India Through Hindu Categories.* New Delhi: Sage.

Marriott, McKim. 1989. "Constructing an Indian ethnosociology", *Contributions to Indian Sociology,* 23,1:1-40

Marx, A. W. 1998) *Making Race and Nation: A Comparison of the United States, South Africa and Brazil.* Cambridge: Cambridge University Press.

Miles, R. 1991. *Racism.* New York: Routledge.

Miles, R. 1993. *Racism after Race Relations.* New York: Routledge.

Modood, T., Berthoud, R. and Nazroo, J. 2000. "Race, Racism and Ethnicity", *Sociology* 36,2:419-427.

Mukherji, U.N. 1909. *Hindus: A Dying Race,* Calcutta.

Nanda, Meera. 2002. *Breaking the Spell of Dharma and Other Essays.* New Delhi: Three Essays Press.

Nanda, Meera. 2003. *Prophets Facing Backwards: Postmodern Critiques of Science and Hindu Nationalism in India.* London: Rutgers University Press.

Nandy, A. 1985. "An Anti-Secularist Manifesto", *Seminar,* October.

Nandy, Ashis. 1987a. *Traditions, Tyranny and Utopias: Essays in the Politics of Awareness.* Delhi: Oxford University Press.

Nandy, Ashis. 1987b. "The Sociology of Sati", *Indian Express,* 5 October, 1987.

Nandy, Ashis. 1988. *Science, Hegemony and Violence: A Requiem for Modernity.* Delhi: Oxford University Press.

Nandy, Ashis. 1992. "Secularism", *Seminar,* June 1992.

Nussbaum, Martha. 2000. "Women and Work: The Capabilities Approach", *The Little Magazine* Vol. 1. No. 1.

Nussbaum, Martha. 2003. "Genocide in Gujarat: The International Community Looks Away", *Dissent* Summer Issue.

Omi, M. and Winant, H. 1994. *Racial Formation in the United States.* New York: Routledge.

Omvedt, G. 2001. "The UN, Racism and Caste", *The Hindu,* 11 April 2001.

Owens, Raymond L. and Nandy, Ashis. 1977. *The New Vaisyas.* Bombay: Allied.

Pandey, G. 1993. "The Civilized and the Barbarian: The 'New' Politics of Late Twentieth Century India and the World" in G. Pandey (ed.) *Hindus and Others: The Question of Identity in India Today.* New Delhi: Viking.

Pandey, Gyanendra. *The Construction of Communalism in Colonial North India.* Delhi: Oxford University Press, 1990.

Pandian, M.S.S. (nd) "Race and Caste", unpublished manuscript on www.uiowa.edu/~intl/ACAD/sasp/SASPBeyond_DurbanPAPERS.html

Panikkar, K.N. 2004. "Protohistory of Hindutva", *The Hindu*, March 02, 2005.

Patterson, O. 1998. *Rituals of Blood: Consequences of Slavery in Two American Centuries.* New York: Basic.

Pollock, S. 1993. "Ramayana and Political Imagination in India", *Journal of Asian Studies*, 52,2:261-197.

Rai, A.S. 1995. "India On-Line: Electronic Bulletin Boards and the construction of a diasporic Hindu Identity", *Diaspora,* 4,1:31-57.

Ratcliffe, P. (ed.) 1994. *Ethnicity and Nation: International Perspectives on Social Conflict.* London: University College London Press.

Ray, Ashwini K. 1993. "India's New Secular Activism: Exploding Some Myths", *Economic and Political Weekly,* May 15:968-973.

Raychaudhuri, Tapan. *2000.* "Shadows of the Swastika: Historical Perspectives on the Politics of Hindu Communalism", *Modern Asian Studies 34,2:259-279.*

Rex, J. 1970. "The Concept of Race in Sociological Theory", in Sami Zubaida (ed.) *Race and Racialism.* London: Tavistock.

Roediger, D.R. 1992. *The Wages of Whiteness: Race and the Making of the American Working Class.* New York: Verso.

Roediger, D.R. 1994. *Towards the Abolition of Whiteness: Essays on Race, Politics and Working Class History.* New York: Verso.

Said, E. 1978. *Orientalism.* London: Routledge and Kegan Paul.

Sarda, H.B. 1906. *Hindu Superiority: An Attempt to Determine the Position of the Hindu Race in the Scale of Nations.* Ajmer: Rajputana Press.

Sarkar, S. 1996. "Indian Nationalism and the Politics of Hindutva", in David Ludden (ed.) *Contesting the Nation.* Philadelphia: University of Pennsylvania Press.

Savarkar, V.D. 1969. *Hindutva: Who is a Hindu?* Bombay.

Sen, A. 1996. "Secularism and its Discontents", in Kaushik Basu and Sanjaya Subramaniam (eds.) *Unravelling the Nation: Sectarian Conflict and India's Secular Identity.* New Delhi: Penguin.

Sen, Amartya. 1993. "Threats to Indian Secularism", *New York Review of Books,* April 8.

Sen, Amartya. 1996. "Secularism and its Discontents", in Kaushik Basu and Sanjay Subramaniam (ed.) *Unravelling the Nation: Sectarian Conflict and India's Secular Identity.* New Delhi: Penguin.

Sethi, Harsh. 1992. "Review of S. Gopal (ed.) *Anatomy of a Confrontation*" in *Seminar,* June 1992.

Shah, Ghanshyam. 1994. "Identity, Communal Consciousness and Politics", *Economic and Political Weekly,* May 7, 1994:1133-1140.

Sharma, J. 2003. *Hindutva: Exploring the Idea of Hindu Nationalism.* New Delhi: Viking.

Sinha, M. 1995. *Colonial Masculinity: The Manly Englishman and the Effeminate Bengali in the late Nineteenth Century.* Manchester: Manchester University Press.

Smith, K. 2002. "Some Critical Observations on the Use of the Concept of Ethnicity in Modood et. al., *Ethnic Minorities in Britain*" *Sociology,* 36,2:399-417.

Solomos, J. and Back, L. 1994. "Conceptualizing Racisms: Social Theory, Politics and Research", *Sociology* 28,1:143-161.

Srinivas, M.N. 1993. "Towards a New Philosophy", *The Times of India*, July 9, 1993.

Strayer, Joseph. *Medieval Statecraft and the Perspective of History*. Princeton: Princeton University Press, 1971.

Talbot, C. 1995. "Inscribing the Other, Inscribing the Self: Hindu-Muslim Relations in Pre-Colonial India", *Comparative Studies in Society and History*, 37,4:692-722.

Talbot, Cynthia. 1995. "Inscribing the Other, Inscribing the Self: Hindu-Muslim Identities in Pre-Colonial India", *Comparative Studies in Society and History* , 37,4:692-722.

Tambiah, S. 1996. *Leveling Crowds: Ethnonationalist Conflict and Collective Violence in India.* Berkeley: University of California Press.

Thapar, Romila. 1971. "The Image of the Barbarian in Early India", *Comparative Studies in Society and History,* 13,4:420-432.

——. 1989. "Imagined Religious Communities? Ancient History and the Modern Search for a Hindu Identity", *Modern Asian Studies,* 23,2:215-225.

——. 1989. "Imagined Religious Communities? Ancient History and the Modern Search for Hindu Identities", *Modern Asian Studies,* 23,2:215-225

Thapar, R., Mukhia, H , and Chandra, B. 1969. *Communalism and the Writing of Indian History.* Delhi: Peoples' Publishing.

Thompson, E.P. 1992. "In the Gentlemen's Cause: The Irish Layer in the Silences of Edmund Burke", *The Times Literary Supplement,* December 4.

Tocqueville, Alexis de. *The Old Regime and the French Revolution.* Garden City. NY: Doubleday, 1955.

Trautmann, T. R. 1997. *Aryans and British India.* Berkeley: University of California Press.

Upadhyaya, P. 1992. "The Politics of Indian Secularism", *Modern Asian*

Studies 26,4:815-54.

van der Veer, Peter. 1988. *Gods on Earth: The Management of Religious Experience and Identity in a North Indian Pilgrimage Centre*. London: Athlone Press.

van der Veer, Peter. 1994. *Religious Nationalism: Hindus and Muslims in India*. Berkeley: University of California Press.

Vanaik, A. 1997. *The Furies of Indian Communalism: Religion, Modernity and Secularization*. New York: Verso.

Varshney, Ashutosh. 2002. *Ethnic Conflict and Civic Life: Hindus and Muslims in India*. New Haven: Yale University Press.

Vivekananda, S. 1993. *Letters of Swami Vivekananda*. Calcutta: Advaita Ashram.

——. [1955] 1962. *The Complete Works of Vivekananda*, 8 Volumes. Calcutta: Advaita Ashram.

——. 1972. *The Complete Works of Swami Vivekananda*. 8 Volumes. Calcutta: Advaita Ashram.

Wacquant, L. "Toward an Analytic of Racial Domination", *Political Power and Social Theory*, 11:221-234.

Wallerstein, I. 1991. "Social Conflict in Post-Independence Black Africa: The Concepts of Race and Status-Group Reconsidered", in E. Balibar and I. Wallerstein, *Race, Nation and Class*. New York: Verso.

——. 1989. "Imagined Religious Communities? Ancient History and the Modern Search for Hindu Identities", *Modern Asian Studies*, 23,2:215-225. "The Construction of Peoplehood: Racism, Nationalism, Ethnicity" in E. Balibar and I. Wallerstein, *Race, Nation, Class*. New York: Verso.

Weber, Max "Politics as a Vocation" in Hans Gerth and C. Wright Mills (ed.) *From Max Weber: Essays in Sociology*. New York: Oxford University Press, 1958.

Wievorika, M. 1995. *The Arena of Racism*. London: Sage.

Wilson, Bryan. 1969. *Religion in a Secular Society*. Harmondsworth: Penguin, 1969.

Wilson, Bryan. 1982. *Religion in Sociological Perspective*. Oxford: Oxford University Press, 1982.

Zeitlin, Irving M. *Ideology and the Development of Sociological Theory*. Englewood Cliffs, NJ: Prentice Hall, 1994.